The
Mormon
Tabernacle
Choir

THE MORMON TABERNACLE CHOIR

Text by Charles Jeffrey Calman

Color Photography by William I. Kaufman

HARPER & ROW, PUBLISHERS
NEW YORK

Cambridge		London
Hagerstown		Mexico City
Philadelphia		São Paulo
San Francisco	*1817*	Sydney

Permission to reproduce photographs is gratefully acknowledged: The Public
Communications Department of the The Church of Jesus Christ of Latter-
day Saints for pictures on pages viii, 108, 110, 112, 162, 164, 175 (Eldon
Linschoten, photographer); 96, 103, 104, 114 (Jerry D. Harvey, photographer); 80, 185 (Jed Clark, photographer); 165 (Eric W. White, photographer);
28 (Marilyn Erd, photographer); 106 (Longin Lonczyna, Jr., photographer);
1 (Craig Law, photographer); color photos 1 and 8 (Eric White, photogra-
pher); xii, 13, 37, 40, 62, 68, 82, 90, 94.
The Photographic Archives, Historical Department, The Church of Jesus Christ
of Latter-day Saints for pictures on pages 8 (from a painting by Lee Greene
Richard), 14 bottom, 31, 34 top, 48 (C. R. Savage, photographer); 34 bottom
(C. W. Carter, photographer); 56 (Sansbury & Johnson, photographers); 6,
10, 14 top, 32, 38, 42, 46, 52, 59, 78
Utah State Historical Society for the picture on page 20.
Saans Photography for the picture on page x.
Deseret News for the picture on page 98 (Jerald Silver, photographer).
Artists whose work accompanies the hymns: Louise Olson, page 121; Virginia
Look, page 126; W. J. Haynie, page 134. Page 154 is from a painting by C. C. A.
Christensen.

Grateful acknowledgment is made to the family of Richard Evans for permission
to excerpt a speech from "Music and the Spoken Word," in *Faith in the Future*
by Richard L. Evans, published by Harper & Row.
The music and hymns appearing on pages 122, 124, 127, 130, 132, 135, 148, 150,
152, 155, 158, and 160 are reprinted from *Hymns*, copyright © 1948 by the
Corporation of the President of The Church of Jesus Christ of Latter-day
Saints. Used by permission. "Easter Morn" by Robert Cundick is used by
permission of The Church of Jesus Christ of Latter-day Saints.

FIRST EDITION

Designed by Lydia Link

Library of Congress Cataloging in Publication Data

Calman, Charles Jeffrey.
  The Mormon Tabernacle Choir.
  Includes index.
  1. Salt Lake City. Tabernacle. Choir. I. Title.
ML200.8.S18T23   783.8'09792'25   79-1656
ISBN 0-06-010624-7

79 80 81 82 83 10 9 8 7 6 5 4 3 2 1

DEDICATED TO THE

Salt Lake Mormon Tabernacle Choir

AND TO OUR UTAH "FAMILIES":

Dr. and Mrs. Allan Barker, Mr. and Mrs. Stephen Case,
Mr. and Mrs. Jack Crofts, Mr. and Mrs. Kent Dastrup,
Dr. and Mrs. David Egli, Mr. and Mrs. Noel Enniss,
Mr. and Mrs. Oakley Evans, Mr. and Mrs. Joseph Gasser,
Mr. and Mrs. Jay Hartvigsen, Mr. and Mrs. Dean Hill,
Mr. and Mrs. Charles Hillier, Mr. and Mrs. Jim Kennard,
Mr. and Mrs. Dale Madsen, Mr. and Mrs. Richard Mueller,
Mr. and Mrs. Noel Taylor, Mr. and Mrs. Kenneth Zeeman

Contents

President and Mrs. Spencer W. Kimball

An Appreciation

CONTEMPLATING the long history of the Salt Lake Mormon Tabernacle Choir, one is led to agree with philosophers and poets that music is well said to be the speech of angels and the universal language of mankind.

The Tabernacle Choir was born in a time of struggle. When despair might well have conquered hope, the first lofty strains of its inspired music nurtured the faith of an isolated, misunderstood people. Today it would be difficult to circumscribe the limits of its influence. The great and moving harmonies of the Tabernacle Choir seem to create a musical common denominator for many faiths, many people.

We are grateful for the Salt Lake Mormon Tabernacle Choir's gift of music and are inspired by the devotion and talent of the Choir's directors, organists, and members. We borrow words from William Wordsworth to express our appreciation:

> The music in my heart I bore
> Long after it was heard no more.

Spencer W. Kimball
President,
The Church of Jesus Christ of Latter-day Saints

Oakley S. Evans

Preface

WHEN JEFF CALMAN approached the Choir with the plan for this book we were very pleased. Ours is a fascinating and inspiring story, well worth the telling.

The Tabernacle Choir was born in a civilization which a small group of pioneers created in the valley of the Great Salt Lake. Even in the hardest of times, these men and women found a place and a time for beauty and music. In a rugged and often inhospitable land, a cultural life unequaled in the west sprang forth as the desert blossomed. As the population of the Territory grew, so did the Choir's size and its reputation. The Choir is representative of the best we have become.

Concert tours have allowed the Choir to meet music lovers in Europe, Japan, and throughout the Americas; our broadcasts and television and motion picture appearances have been seen and heard around the world. The Choir has been in the forefront of new means of communications, from our earliest recordings in 1910 and our first broadcasts, to the first experiments with stereophonic sound, long-playing records, and the inaugural television relay across the Atlantic by satellite.

This year, we celebrated the golden anniversary of our weekly broadcast, "Music and the Spoken Word," America's oldest network program. Although we are proud of these achievements, we do not expect to rest on our laurels.

We value this book's insights into both our history and the Choir of today. Jeff Calman has told the Choir's story eloquently, and has caught the essence of our spirit.

Oakley S. Evans
President
The Salt Lake Mormon Tabernacle Choir

Jerold D. Ottley

Introduction

THE TABERNACLE CHOIR is made up of dedicated volunteers from every walk of life who come together to sing to the people of the world. It is this sense of communication, spirit to spirit, singer to listener, which energizes the Choir.

Although The Church of Jesus Christ of Latter-day Saints sponsors the Choir, we perform primarily in the secular world. Our challenge is to reach out through music, sharing with our fellow men our rich spiritual heritage.

We have an obligation to raise our level of musicianship, to broaden the range of the music we sing, to participate in the mainstream of contemporary American musical life. The musical staff is dedicated to making the Choir one of the most respected organizations in music. This is a challenging task. Music which appeals to professional musicians may not always please the general public.

We hope to be recognized as a group which presents high-quality music, extremely well sung, to a broad and varied audience. We also want to provide an exciting and ever-changing kaleidoscope of musical experiences which our listeners will find both musically and spiritually moving.

Twelve men, each with his own character and talent, have preceded me to this podium, a perspective which is at once encouraging and intimidating. But I am blessed with choice associates. We are a team as musicians and as individuals. Most of all, we appreciate the members of the Choir, whose talents and devotion are the essence of what the Choir has always been. Their singing causes me to echo the sentiments expressed by Brigham Young, more than 100 years ago:

> . . . Some wise being organized my system, and gave me my capacity, put into my heart and brain something that delights, charms, and fills me with rapture at the sound of sweet music. . . . It was the Lord, our Heavenly Father, who gave me the capacity to enjoy these sounds, and which we ought to do in His name, and to His glory!

Jerold D. Ottley
Conductor
The Salt Lake Mormon Tabernacle Choir

Note

THE SPARK that sent me on the road to Salt Lake City was a friend's comment that the Mormon Tabernacle Choir would complete fifty years of radio broadcasting in July 1979. After so many years of national and international prominence for the Choir, it seemed only right that a book should finally celebrate their contribution and history. Harper & Row agreed.

When the officials of the Mormon Tabernacle Choir consented to cooperate on such a book, I could hardly have expected the total cooperation and the unusual life experience I would come to have. Since I knew very little about The Church of Jesus Christ of Latter-day Saints, I asked to live with different members of the Choir while in Salt Lake City. And, so, every Thursday night after Choir rehearsal, I went to live with a new family for the week—learning not only about the Choir and the Mormon faith, but also observing their life-style, their joy in work and family, and their love for music.

Looking back on the experience, I realize I was privy to a special treasure of love, kindness, and understanding. Hailing from New York and a different faith, I wanted to do a book on the Mormon Tabernacle Choir because of its place in American music and history. The objective, however, was transcended by interaction with many who truly became "brothers and sisters," an association I will always hold sacred.

It is my wish that you, the reader, take from this book the knowledge of the Choir and the spirit of their music that will enable you, also, to share in a common bond.

Charles Jeffrey Calman

Acknowledgments

THIS BOOK is the sum total of the cooperation of many people. I thank everyone for his help and ask forgiveness if, by error, I have omitted anyone.

Maestro Maurice Abravanel, Kristene Allen, Gary Alvey, Marion Arave, Dr. Leonard J. Arrington, Veloy W. Bailey, Meredith Barker, Jerry P. Cahill, Ann L. Cannaday, Bruce Carneal, William D. Carpenter, Jim Christensen, Jed A. Clark, Dr. Richard P. Condie, Patrick J. Coppin, J. Spencer Cornwall, Margaret H. Cragun, Dr. Robert Cundick, Roy M. Darley, Erin W. Davis, Bob deWitt, Melvin W. Dunn, Marilyn Erd, Oakley S. Evans, Paul H. Evans, Mrs. Richard L. Evans, Dr. Harvey Fletcher, Mr. and Mrs. Paul A. Foulger, Thomas Frost, Charles R. Gibbs, Dr. F. Charles Graves, Elizabeth Haglund, Alice Haycock, Jeanie Haynie, Helen R. Hillier, Colleen Hinckley, W. Kennedy Hodges, Frederick M. Huchel, Mary Jack, J. J. Keeler, David Kern, Edward B. Kimball, James L. Kimball, J. Spencer Kinard, John G. Kinnear, Joan Kleinman, Staff of KSL, Brent A. Lawrence, Eldon K. Linschoten, Dr. John T. Longhurst, Warren F. Luch, Harold Lundstrom, Sherman Martin, Richard L. Merrell, James Mortimer, Phyllis D. Mossing, Ruth Nash, Merriloy P. Niederer, Emma R. Olsen, Laurie Olson, Richard G. Oman, Maestro Eugene Ormandy, Dr. Jerold D. Ottley, JoAnn Ottley, Sadie H. Parker, Bob Passey, Udell E. Poulsen, Mick Reasor, Dr. Donald H. Ripplinger, E. Dennis Rowley, Dr. Lorry E. Rytting, Dr. Alexander Schreiner, Russell Scott, William W. Slaughter, Jenae Smith, Marian R. Smith, Dr. Melvin T. Smith, Rolland F. Sparks, Mary Loo Stephens, Shirley M. Stoddard, Mr. and Mrs. Clark N. Stohl, Alice Swensen, Mamie Talbot, Blanche Tippon, Nelson Wadsworth, Bettie L. Walker, Janet C. Watson, Dr. Lorin F. Wheelwright, Eric W. White, Sarah White, Amelda Wilcox, and Dr. Heber G. Wolsey.

And to Jay Mitchell, Maida Milchen, Tim Christy, Terri Blender, Carol Zito, George Moskowitz, Gloria Patterson, A. B. Allen, Sandberg and Hochstein, and, most of all, Gwen DeLuca, special appreciation for their gracious efforts and good humor.

I am grateful to Professor Jim Christensen for his help and guidance and to the following members of the Art Department of Brigham Young University for their illustrations in this volume: Bob deWitt, Jeanie Haynie, Colleen Hinckley, David Kearn, Laurie Olson, Bob Passey, Mick Reasor, and Jenae Smith.

The Salt Lake City Mormon Tabernacle

I

The Singing Saints

A RUDE BUZZING from the clock radio reminds Gordon and Bonnie Rae Bigler that the short night is at an end. It has only been a few hours since they closed their fast-food restaurant in Brigham City, and now, through squinting eyelids, Gordon confirms the time: 5:00 (A.M.). Only a few dairy farmers are up this early in the northern Utah community of Mantua, especially on Sunday.

No other traffic is on the highway as the Biglers point their blue 1973 Ford LTD sedan down the canyon toward Interstate 15 and Salt Lake City, sixty miles away. En route, they stop for Oakley Moore in Brigham City and John White in Willard before picking up Linda Burns and Raydell Cobia in Roy. It has been two days since they last made this trip together, and the car radio is turned down while they exchange new stories of family and friends.

South of Salt Lake City, attorney Richard Taylor leaves his home in Spanish Fork at 6:05 A.M. and travels along I-15 for a rendezvous in Orem with Kathy Visher, Elfriede Poecker, Lois Johnson, Orvilla Stevens, and Susan Clough. (Mrs. Taylor has figured out that her husband spends more time each week visiting with the five ladies in the car pool than he does with her.)

For two years before the Stephen Boyds moved to Provo, they were making the same pilgrimage two or three times a week from Evanston, 85 miles away in Wyoming, traveling over 17,000 miles a year. Now they travel only half that distance. After being transferred from Salt Lake City to Mesa, Arizona, R. Dwight Laws made the trip from one to three times each week by jet. In eighteen months, he piled up an estimated 230,000 air miles.

While some will catch what sleep they can along the way, others are beginning what seems a terrible crime against nature—loosening up their vocal cords with those exercises which singers perform without self-consciousness only when they are with other singers or by themselves.

The nine children of cancer surgeon Merrill Wilson and his wife, LaRae, have learned to sleep through this routine. Though they live in Salt Lake City itself, Sundays still begin at 5:00 A.M., the same time Dr. Wilson begins his gardening on summer weekdays. Later, the children will prepare their own breakfast, and then get themselves, including Phillip, age four, to Sunday School on time.

For each member of the Choir, it is a routine he or she may have repeated as many as 129 times in a single year, with a cost to some of thousands of dollars. In couples, groups, and singly they drive—only a few live close enough to walk—through the quiet streets of Salt Lake City. In the winter months it will still be dark when they arrive in time to change clothes and be in their assigned seats at 7:45 A.M.

Their destination is the dome-shaped Tabernacle on Temple Square in the heart of Salt Lake City. They have an appointment to keep, a weekly ritual repeated by them and their predecessors for fifty years. They are the Singing Saints, members of the Salt Lake Mormon Tabernacle Choir, and their date is with Tabernacle visitors and an audience of loyal radio listeners and television viewers.

Before the half-hour broadcast goes out over the airwaves, conductor, organist, singers, and a host of technicians will have been making preparations for almost two hours, the result of which will be introduced by these words: "Once more, we welcome you within these walls, with Music and the Spoken Word from the crossroads of the West. . . ." Another radio and television broadcast by the Mormon Tabernacle Choir has begun. The 300 Choir members are a spreading fan of color, bright blue against the warm gold and brown of the mighty Tabernacle organ. Towering behind the performers are the organ's thirty-two-foot pipes, glinting under the television lights. As the Choir and organ reach a climax of sound, the organist will depress a pedal releasing air into the thirty-two-foot stops, and the floors of a building seating 6,000 will throb.

Every week, thousands of visitors from around the world attend the broadcast. There is no applause after individual selections. Although the Salt Lake Tabernacle is neither church nor chapel, audiences hesitate to applaud. Many feel that they are in a sacred place, attending a worship service; for them, the broadcast transcends ordinary musical experience. For perhaps millions across America, the Sunday broadcast is the only "church" they attend each week—their few minutes of quiet meditation about the meaning of their lives.

In a tradition now half a century old, an announcer's calm but earnest voice has briefly discussed a question of morals or values, of honesty or simple good behavior. Before and after his message, the Choir has sung. Theirs is an exciting sound, controlled yet overwhelming in its impact. It has been a varied program, music by Mozart or Brahms, a hymn, a folk song, a work by a contemporary Utah composer. "Music and the Spoken Word" is one of the few live network radio programs, along with news and sports, left on the air, and radio's oldest weekly coast-to-coast program by an American musical organization.

People join the Choir most often because they love to sing. All are volunteers, who may devote more than fifteen hours each week to it. While their rewards include prestige, warm friendships, and glorious reminiscences of "singing with the Philadelphia Orchestra," the biggest reward is the joy of service: to self, to their fellow man, to God. Remembering the impact their singing sometimes has on people's lives, they enjoy moments of realization which are reason enough for the sacrifices Choir membership requires. Their devotion comes across to every audience, enabling members to join in a world-changing good, by doing what they most love to do: making music.

Every singer is a member of The Church of Jesus Christ of Latter-day Saints, which encourages music-making at home as well as in church. In both, it is an extension of prayer and an expression of love for others. In the local congregations music is a community activity, which leads organists, choir leaders, and singers to join together to make music on Sunday mornings and evenings, developing their talents and praising the Creator.

Joseph Smith, Jr., founder and first Prophet of the Church, concluded his declaration of faith with these words: "If there is anything virtuous, lovely, or of good report or praiseworthy, we seek after these things." The cultural arts, being both lovely and of good report, entered early into the mainstream of Mormon life, and today the Tabernacle Choir represents a pinnacle of achievement for music-loving Mormons.

The Choir was originally founded to provide music for the General Conferences of the Church, convocations of Church leadership and membership which take place twice a year. Over the last fifty years, however, the weekly broadcast concert has come to be the most important activity of the Choir, one which has considerable, often uncalculated, impact.

Sacred music chosen for broadcast by conductor Jerold Ottley is performed in the months that follow by church choirs of many denominations throughout the land. Other selections will soon be recorded for release in new Tabernacle Choir albums (the Choir is surpassed only by the illustrious New York Philharmonic and Philadelphia orchestras as the best-selling classical artists on the Columbia Masterworks record label), or find their way onto the concert program of an impending tour in countries as far away as Japan.

These Utah housewives, schoolteachers, businessmen, surgeons, and welders comprise the world's largest concert ensemble, performing to sold-out houses in the major cities of North America, Europe, and the Orient. And to ensure its continuance, in the last decade an innovative program was launched to provide a supply of experienced young choral singers to replace those who retire from service.

That such a cultural phenomenon is maintained today at the "Crossroads of the West" is commendable. That it was spawned—and that it survived—in a harsh land which initially was beyond the borders of the United States is astounding.

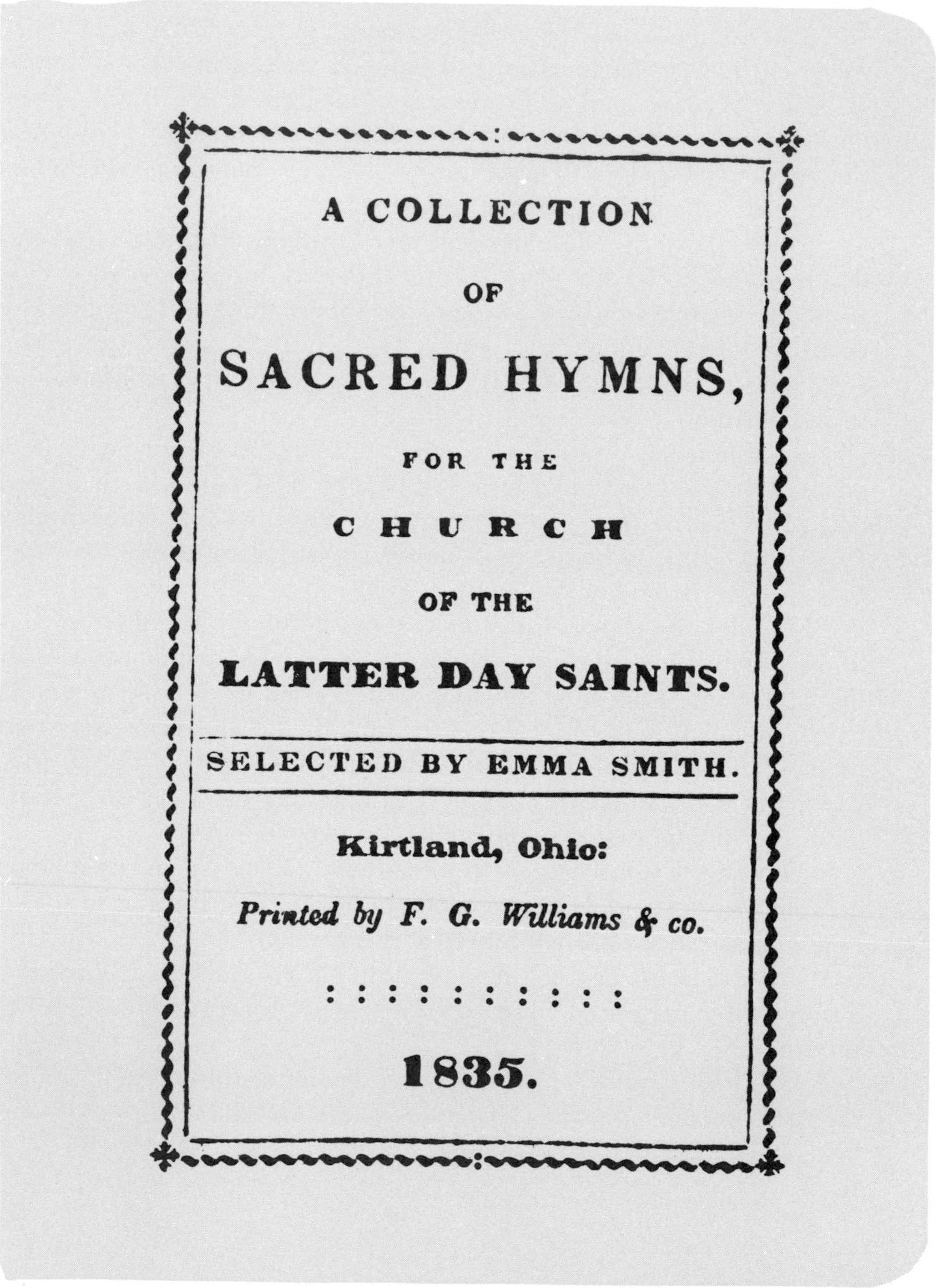

A COLLECTION

OF

SACRED HYMNS,

FOR THE

CHURCH

OF THE

LATTER DAY SAINTS.

SELECTED BY EMMA SMITH.

Kirtland, Ohio:

Printed by F. G. Williams & co.

: : : : : : : : : :

1835.

Title page from the first edition of Emma Smith's hymn collection

2

Beginnings

There is no music in hell, for all good music belongs to heaven. Sweet harmonious sounds give exquisite joy to human beings capable of appreciating music. I delight in hearing harmonious tunes made by the human voice, any musical sound that can be made belongs to the Saints and is for the Saints.

—Brigham Young, March 6, 1862

EARLY MORMON COMMUNITIES were marked not only by order, industry, and rapid growth, but also by a reverence for literature, music, and art which made them seem strangely out of place on America's frontier. Unlike the towns started by the trappers and traders, the prospectors and prostitutes, the cowboys and sheep men, Mormon settlements were planned, permanent communities with a sophistication and culture more akin to the country's oldest and proudest cities.

The arts graced their homes in each new settlement. When uprooted and driven farther west, they managed to preserve the cultural arts for the rising generation. Convert immigrants from Great Britain, Scandinavia, and Europe enriched their cultural lives with Old World flavor.

Finally, in the high valleys of the Rocky Mountains, Brigham Young colonized an intermountain empire in which there soon flourished a rich variety of home-grown drama and serious music. In this climate, one of the world's notable musical organizations, the Tabernacle Choir, was to be born and nurtured.

During the 1820s, in western New York State, revival singing was an important part of the religious excitement which led to the establishment of The Church of Jesus Christ of Latter-day Saints. And when, on April 6, 1830, Joseph Smith, Jr., assembled his followers to formally incorporate the Church, hymn-singing was made part and parcel of that and succeeding services.

Emma Smith

Joseph Smith loved music, often singing ballads and hymns in times of personal stress and discouragement, and in worship he encouraged his people to join him in song. There was as yet no distinctively Mormon music, and those who came to worship sang the Protestant hymns in general usage.

In Harmony, Pennsylvania, four months after Smith established the Church, the Prophet announced a revelation from the Lord to Joseph's wife, Emma:

> And verily I say unto thee that thou shalt lay aside the things of this world, and seek for the things of a better.
>
> And it shall be given thee, also, to make a selection of sacred hymns, as it shall be given thee, which is pleasing unto me, to be had in my church.
>
> For my soul delighteth in the song of the heart; yea, the song of the righteous is a prayer unto me, and it shall be answered with a blessing upon their heads.
>
> —Doctrine and Covenants 25:10-12

The third paragraph is a key to understanding the place music has in Mormondom. Regarded as modern scripture by the Latter-day Saints, the declaration of the Lord's delight in "the song of the heart" is a basis for their belief that singing, when offered in righteousness, is a prayer, and that the Lord's blessings will surely follow their offerings of music.

Emma Smith set out to compile the hymnbook: Mormon music had begun. Joseph's wife was a fine musician and had studied voice. (Writing in 1914, Vida E. Smith, the granddaughter of Joseph Smith, reported, "Some now living recall the ease with which she would take the high notes in some of the old-time hymns, even after she had passed late middle-life.")

During the next five years, the Church community moved from New York to Ohio. Although hindered during this time of travail, Emma kept editing, compiling, collecting, and in 1835, her hymnbook was finally completed. It contained no music, nor did she suggest popular tunes or familiar hymn melodies to accompany the poems. Subsequent editions generally identified appropriate tunes. While the Church was still building its repertoire of sacred music, a borrowed tune was usually more acceptable than a borrowed text, since often the poetry of the latter did not represent the revealed theology and worship of what they called the Restored Church.

Emma Smith's new hymnbook contained ninety hymns, thirty-two of which had already appeared in separate Mormon publications—newspapers or journals established wherever Mormons settled. The oldest of these newpapers, *The Evening and Morning Star,* published in Independence, Missouri, in 1832 printed the first Mormon hymns in its premier edition. The founder and editor of the *Star,* William Wine Phelps, was the most important of the early Latter-day Saints hymnists, and twenty-nine of his poems were reprinted in Emma Smith's hymnal, many more than by any other Mormon poet. Most of

William W. Phelps

the remaining hymns were borrowed from popular Protestant anthologies.

A subsequent hymnal was published in 1840, in Manchester, England, by Brigham Young, and an expanded edition of Emma Smith's collection followed in Nauvoo, Illinois, in 1841. The first hymnal with music was published in Bellows Falls, Vermont, in 1844.

One of Phelps's best hymns, "The Spirit of God Like a Fire Is Burning," was sung at the dedication of the sacred Temple in Kirtland, Ohio, on March 27, 1836. The climax of the service was a dedicatory prayer delivered by Joseph Smith. Suddenly, voices of a choir burst forth from the four corners of the temple, singing "The Spirit of God." It was a great moment of liturgical theater. And it was the beginning of the Mormon Choir tradition.

Unlike subsequent temples built by the Church, the Kirtland Temple served as a center for many community functions, including rehearsals and classes. The Kirtland musicians, who sang at the dedication of the Temple, probably became the nucleus of other choirs which were to perform a few years later.

In 1839, following a short-lived and violent settlement attempt among hostile neighbors in Jackson County, Missouri, a new gathering place was selected at the western edge of Illinois, on the east bank of the Mississippi River. Joseph Smith named it Nauvoo, meaning "the beautiful."

Music flourished in Nauvoo. In 1841, a group of singers from the beautiful city by the Mississippi organized America's first university-level music department. Part of the first municipal university in the United States, it was organized under a charter of incorporation which provided: "The City Council may establish and organize an institution of learning within the limits of the city, for the teaching of the Arts, Sciences, and Learned Professions, to be called the University of the City of Nauvoo."

The university's department of music was created to meet popular demand:

> The Choir of singers presented a petition to the Board of Regents of the University at their last sitting for the appointment of a "professor and wardens in the Department of Music in the City of Nauvoo" to constitute a board for the regulation of music in this city, which was adopted, and the following persons appointed to wit:
>
> PROFESSOR   Gustavus Hills
>
> WARDENS
> B. S. Wilbur—First Ward
> Stephen H. Goddard—Second Ward
> Titus Billings—Third Ward
> John Pack—Fourth Ward.

The Chancellor, General John C. Bennett, recommended that the regents instruct the board composed of the professor and wards, aforesaid, to prohibit the *flat* sound of the notes, and adopt the *board,* whereupon General Joseph Smith observed: 'I move the instruction, for I was always opposed to anything *flat.*' The motion prevailed.

———
11

The university's program soon attracted favorable attention. On January 15, 1842, Nauvoo's newspaper, *The Times and Seasons*, editorialized:

> We are pleased to see the laudable zeal manifested by some of our *musical friends*, to bring about a uniform and tasteful style of sacred singing. Among a people emigrated from different countries, with different prejudices and habits as we are, this is no easy task, and we can but admire the improvements made, and the judicious order established within a few months past. By the by, we peeped in the other evening, during the performance of the Musical Lyceum, and heard what will make us try to peep in again.
>
> A proper and expressive articulation of the words constitute the life and soul of music; intelligence thus clothes with the robes of melody, and harmonic numbers, moves gently over the spirit, imprints her heavenly footsteps, and awakens all its energies. We should not be so sure that the performances before hinted at were good, were it not that we are sure we have a tolerably good ear for music, and an ear for good music and we were delighted, whereas our devil, who is known to have a bad ear for good music, and a good ear for bad music, was quite differently affected; he crowded in edgewise, but soon deserted,—said he could not stand the racket.

With over 12,000 residents, Nauvoo soon became one of the largest cities in Illinois. Later, waves of European immigrants, converts to the Church, increased the population by as much as half.

The cultural life of the new community took shape rapidly. While many religious movements during the middle of the nineteenth century frowned on cultural and recreational activities, the Mormons saw music, theater, and even dancing as vehicles for the expression of the very best in man's spiritual life. Music was everywhere, at weddings and on other special occasions. Touring musicians played on street corners. Nauvoo theatricals thrived at a time when other religions were trying to close theaters. Prominent among the performers was Brigham Young, who succeeded Joseph Smith to the leadership of the Church. President Young was a fine singer as well as a dedicated amateur actor.

Along with the dances, balls, and theatrical performances, the development of choir singing, which had begun in Kirtland, was renewed. But the choir had no settled place in which to perform or hold rehearsals, and never attained the honored place of the Nauvoo "band." Officially the "Band of the Nauvoo Legion" (actually, a small orchestra: three violins, a cello, two clarinets, three flutes, two trumpets, and a trombone, all under the baton of "Superintendent of the Orchestra" William Pitt) provided martial music for the maneuvers of the Nauvoo Legion, a regiment of the Illinois State Militia under the command of Lieutenant General Joseph Smith, Jr. Out of uniform, the band provided concert and dance music for public and private occasions.

In public performances, the choir was always eclipsed by the band. On one such occasion, the laying of the cornerstone for the new Temple, both choir and band music were featured. *The Times and Seasons'* note concerning the perform-

The Kirtland Temple

Nauvoo, Illinois (from a contemporary engraving in Charles A. Dana, ed.,
The United States Illustrated)

ance implies the lesser place the choir seemed to hold: "The choir, *also*, under the direction of B. S. Wilbur, deserve commendation."

But the "Holy City of Nauvoo," described by Josiah Quincy Adams as "an orderly city, magnificently laid out and teeming with activity and enterprise," was soon to be no more. The Prophet, Joseph Smith, was killed by mob violence, the city was stormed by its neighbors, and the Saints were forced to move again. Brigham Young, upon whom the Prophet's spiritual and temporal mantle had fallen, began to prepare for the grandest quest in the history of America.

Brigham Young was President of the Council of Twelve Apostles under Joseph Smith and became the second president of The Church of Jesus Christ of Latter-day Saints upon the death of its founder. Brigham shouldered his responsibilities with epic vision and resolve.

By late 1845 the situation in Nauvoo was no longer tenable. The Saints, however, forced once again to abandon their homes, their farms, and their places of work, still found time to sing:

> *Early this spring we'll leave Nauvoo,*
> *And on our journey we'll pursue,*
> *We'll go and bid the mob farewell,*
> *And let them go to heaven or hell.*
>
> *The temple shining silver bright,*
> *And Christ's own glory gives the light,*
> *High on the mountains we will rear*
> *A standard to the nations far.*
>
> REFRAIN:
>
> *So on the way to California*
> *In the spring we'll take our journey,*
> *Far above Arkansas fountains,*
> *Pass between the Rocky Mountains.*

The westward journey would have two legs. From Nauvoo, on the banks of the Mississippi, the Saints moved during 1846 across Iowa to a new staging area on the banks of the Missouri. The trek across the Great Plains was to follow in 1847.

By a stroke of genius which became settled policy, Brigham Young's advance parties always included musicians. The Nauvoo Band was with him in 1846, providing entertainment and sustaining morale. Impromptu public concerts along the way also helped pay for the trip. Half a century later, the Tabernacle Choir would travel along a similar route, paying their expenses from concert receipts.

Band of the Nauvoo Legion

The log huts of Winter Quarters, Nebraska, where Mormon pioneers spent the winter of 1846–47. (Painting by Mormon folk artist C. C. A. Christensen)

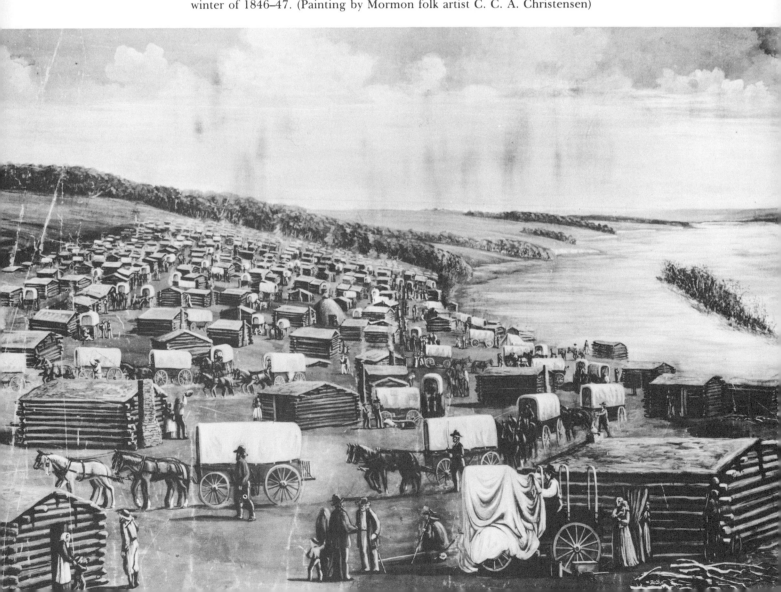

It was during this trip that the best known of all Mormon hymns was composed, the hymn which is requested by Tabernacle Choir audiences more often than any other, which is included in fourteen of the Choir's recordings, and is a perennial broadcast offering. William Clayton, one of the Church's early converts in England, had immigrated to Nauvoo in 1840. Clayton had been secretary to Joseph Smith and kept an extensive journal. On Wednesday, April 15, 1846, he wrote, "This morning I composed a song—'All Is Well.' " Or, "Come, Come, Ye Saints," as it is more generally called. Clayton wrote the hymn in thanksgiving for the birth of a "fine, fat boy" to his wife, Diantha, whom he had left behind in Nauvoo.

"Come, Come, Ye Saints" is typical of so many early Mormon hymns: it is not a completely original piece, rather an adaptation. A hymn entitled "All Is Well" had been published in 1844 in a hymnbook called *The Sacred Harp* and is very similar to "Come, Come, Ye Saints" both in text and melody. In the vast majority of instances, the people who compiled early southern hymnals such as *The Sacred Harp* arranged existing, traditional material, folk songs common to the English-speaking world. It is perhaps most appropriate to conceive of William Clayton's composition and the earlier "All Is Well" as cousins rather than father and son. Adding his own beliefs and aspirations to the oral tradition, William Clayton created an enduring monument to his faith.

Expressing the hopes and expectations of the Mormon pioneers, the hymn also figures prominently in folktales handed down through the generations, the most common of which is that Brigham Young told William Clayton, "I want you to write a hymn that the people can sing at their campfires, in the evening; something that will give them succor and support, and help them to fight the many troubles and trials of the journey."

Heber J. Grant, the seventh President and Prophet of the Church, remembered a story his father-in-law told him which illustrates the hymn's importance in the pioneer camps:

One night, as we were making camp, we noticed one of our brethren had not arrived and a volunteer party was immediately organized to return and see if anything had happened to him. Just as we were about to start, we saw the missing brother coming in the distance. When he arrived he said he had been quite sick; so some of us unyoked his oxen and attended to his part of the camp duties. After supper, he sat down before the campfire on a large rock and sang in a very faint but plaintive and sweet voice, the hymn "Come, Come, Ye Saints." It was a rule of the camp that whenever anybody started this hymn all in the camp should join, but for some reason this evening nobody joined him. He sang the hymn alone. When he had finished I doubt if there was a single dry eye in the camp. The next morning we noticed that he was not yoking up his cattle. We went to his wagon and found that he had died during the night. We dug a shallow grave and after we had covered the body with the earth we rolled the large stone to the head of the grave to mark it—the stone on which he had been sitting the night before when he sang: "And should we die before our journey's through—happy day, all is well."

17

Another glimpse of prairie life at the new base camp comes from Colonel Thomas L. Kane, a Pennsylvania attorney and life-long Presbyterian who became a self-appointed advocate of the Mormons. In 1846 he witnessed the mustering of the Mormon Battalion of 500 men who enlisted to serve in the war with Mexico. The battalion was to complete an overland infantry march of more than 1,500 miles, but would never fire a shot in combat. They rejoined their families in Salt Lake Valley a year later, but not before contributing to the folk music and lore of the Mormons. Kane described the eve of their departure from Iowa:

> The afternoon before was appropriated by a farewell ball; and a more merry dancing rout I have never seen. . . .
>
> With the rest, attended the Elders of the Church within call, including nearly all the chiefs of the High Council, with their wives and children. They, the gravest and most trouble-worn, seemed the most anxious of any to be the first to throw off the burden of heavy thoughts. Their leading off the dancing in a great double cotillion, was the signal bade the festivity commence. To the canto of debonair violins, the cheer of horns, the jingle of sleigh bells, and the jovial snoring of the tambourine, they did dance! None of your minuets or other mortuary processions of gentles in etiquette, tight shoes, and pinching gloves, but the spirited and scientific displays of our venerated and merry grandparents . . . executed with the spirit of people too happy to be slow, or bashful, or constrained. Light hearts, lithe figures, and light feet, had it their own way from an early hour till after the sun had dipped behind the sharp sky-line of the Omaha hills. Silence was then called, and a well cultivated mezzo-soprano voice, belonging to a young lady with fair face and dark eyes, gave with quartette accompaniment a little song, the notes of which I have been unsuccessful in repeated efforts to obtain since—a version of the text, touching to all earthly wanderers:

> > *By the rivers of Babylon we sat down and wept.*
> > *We wept when we remembered Zion.*

> Well as I knew the peculiar fondness of the Mormons for music, their orchestra in service on this occasion astonished me by its numbers and fine drill. The story was, that an eloquent Mormon missionary had converted its members in a body at an English town, a stronghold of the sect, and that they took up their trumpets, trombones, drums, and hautboys together, and followed him to America.

> When the refugees from Nauvoo were hastening to part with their table ware, jewelery, and almost every other fragment of metal wealth they possessed that was not iron, they had never thought of giving up the instruments of this favorite band. And when the battalion was enlisted, though high inducements were offered some of the performers to accompany it, they all refused. Their fortunes were with the camp of the tabernacle. They had led the farewell service in the Nauvoo temple. Their office now was to guide the monster choruses and Sunday hymns; and like the trumpets of silver, made of a whole piece, "for the calling of the assembly, and for the journeying of the camps," to knoll the people into church. Some of their wind instruments, indeed, were uncommonly full and

pure-toned, and in that clear, dry air could be heard to a great distance. It had the strangest effect in the world, to listen to their sweet music winding over the uninhabited country. Something in the style of a Moravian death-tune blown at day-break, but altogether unique. It might be when you were hunting a ford over the great Platte, the dreariest of all wild rivers, perplexed among the far-reaching sand bars, and curlew shallows of its shifting bed—the wind rising would bring you the first faint thought of a melody; and as you listened borne down upon the gust that swept past you a cloud of the dry sifted sands, you recognized it —perhaps a home-loved theme of Henry Proch or Mendelssohn. Mendelssohn Bartholdy, away there in the Indian marches!

The devastating winter of 1846–47 was spent in the log huts of their new settlements on the Missouri River. Then, on April 5, 1847, the first company of pioneers left Winter Quarters, Nebraska, and headed west. Brigham headed the party of 143 men, 3 women, and 2 children toward the valley of the Great Salt Lake. Orson Pratt and Erastus Snow, the company scouts, became the first Mormons to enter the Salt Lake Valley, on July 21, 1847. With the remaining people, Brigham Young entered the valley on July 24. Rising from his wagon sickbed, he looked ahead of him and said, "This is the place!"

The sight was at once welcome and forbidding. It meant both journey's end and new beginnings. Before the carefully husbanded potatoes and corn could be planted, the streams would have to be dammed and the sun-baked soil moistened, softened, and turned. And before the Saints could assemble in conference, a Bowery would have to be constructed to provide protection from the midsummer sun. Even so, within four weeks of their arrival, the first General Conference to be held in Utah would be convened and another seed planted which, with care and nurturing, would become the Tabernacle Choir.

The Old Tabernacle in Salt Lake

3

Songs of Zion

THE VANGUARD had arrived. Behind them, spaced weeks and hundreds of miles apart, other wagon trains were already etching ever deeper the trail of the Mormon pioneers. A second company arrived July 29, with their own indelible memories of life and music on the trail, singing by day, dancing and fiddle-playing at night. Erastus Snow had written in his diary, "As I write I hear the sound of music and dancing on the other side of the circle. This is a very common recreation in camp, though we have to dispense with the ladies, a very great *desideratum.*"

In the twenty-two years before the coming of the railroad in 1869, 80,000 Mormons crossed the plains, the majority of them walking or pulling handcarts. Among these were several destined to become instrumental in the development of Mormon music, including George Careless, Ebenezer Beesley, and Evan Stephens.

In their first month in the valley of the Great Salt Lake, the settlers staked a claim on the land in the name of the United States and called it by the name Deseret, from a *Book of Mormon* reference to the honeybee. The beehive emblem and the motto, "Industry," retained even today, were certainly appropriate. An adobe fort, built as a defense against possible Indian attack, included the homes of Brigham Young and Heber C. Kimball, his First Counselor. Yet in this city, which had barely begun to be built, the Mormons took time to pray and create a choir.

The Mormon Tabernacle Choir first sang on August 22, 1847 (twenty-nine days after the pioneers had entered the Salt Lake Valley) at the first General Conference to be held in Utah. At that time, there were fewer settlers in the valley than there are singers in today's Choir, and, since there were not many women, few female singers. In fact the Choir was so small it needed no conductor. The Choir had no name and the Tabernacle was twenty years away from being built.

It was this Choir, nonetheless, which began the tradition of a mighty Salt Lake Choir and continued the legacy of music the pioneers brought with them.

The Conference met in the Bowery, built by a contingent of the Mormon Battalion after their arrival July 29. It stood on one corner of a ten-acre square on which a new Temple would eventually stand. The four walls of the Bowery were of adobe, its roof built from tree boughs and earth, supported by posts. Forty feet long by twenty-eight feet wide, it could hold approximately 1,000 people. It was at this Conference that the community was named the City of the Great Salt Lake. (The name was changed to Great Salt Lake City in 1851, and the "Great" was dropped years later.)

According to the minutes of the Conference, the Choir sang "The Spirit of God Like a Fire Is Burning" and a Protestant hymn by Isaac Watts, "From All That Dwell Below the Skies," a versification of Psalm 117. There was, as yet, no organ or keyboard instrument in Salt Lake City, but wind or string instruments probably accompanied the singers at the General Conference. And in only a few years, the transplanted Nauvoo Band would again perform with the Choir.

By 1850, only three years after it was founded, Salt Lake City already had a population of 11,380. The 1847 Bowery was replaced by a larger one within two years, and the first Tabernacle was built two years later, in 1851. Its permanent roof of wooden shingles covered walls of adobe block, a stone foundation, a congregation of 2,500, and, eventually, Joseph Ridges's first pipe organ, comprising what is now known as the Old Tabernacle. Finally, in 1867, the present Tabernacle, with a new organ, became the Choir's permanent home. Meanwhile, the Choir made its first appearance outside of General Conference, participating in the ceremony of laying the four cornerstones of the Temple.

Not all Mormon settlers stayed in Salt Lake City. Beginning the first summer, Brigham Young fostered and directed the establishment of other communities, 15, 40, even 100 miles away. A colony was sent to San Bernardino, California, as early as 1851. Every effort was made to make each new community self-sufficient and viable by selecting individuals with the necessary skills: carpenters, managers, farmers, storekeepers, and, remembering earlier experiences, teachers and musicians. In 1861, for example, a group of 132 adults was assigned to settle what is now St. George, 300 miles south of Salt Lake City. Five of them were musicians, providing entertainment, building morale, and serving the Lord with song by establishing local choirs.

Immigrants came into the Salt Lake Valley only to leave immediately for a small town, newly begun, clinging to the edge of wilderness. Many brought fresh musical talent, and groups leaving the city to found a new settlement sometimes even delayed their departure hoping that a good baritone or soprano would be among the arrivals. One bishop let it be known that he would offer ten acres of his town's best land if a good tenor would settle and agree to sing in his ward's choir. (The ward is the local congregation of the LDS Church organization.)

The citizens formed choirs and bands to perform not only in church, but also for concerts, for public celebrations, for funerals; some established music schools. These small-town choirs often performed amazingly sophisticated music. In Parowan, a southern Utah town of only a few hundred residents, the choir and a small band performed movements from a Haydn mass—in Latin! In another town young and old alike went to singing classes. John Taylor of Provo was paid ten dollars a week to give band lessons. When President Young traveled to one of the outlying communities, banners and the town band would greet him at the outskirts, and the musicians would serenade him to the town square, playing for him again when he left to continue his journey.

The thriving cultural life of Salt Lake City in the early 1850s is evidence of the social forces which led to a continuation of a choral tradition throughout this early, difficult period. Nearby, but separated from Temple Square, two other public buildings were rising to accommodate the social and cultural life of the booming community. First was the Social Hall, where, starting in 1852, dancing, concerts, theatrical events, and Choir rehearsals were scheduled.

The second was the Salt Lake Theatre. Its dedication, on March 6, 1862, as a new home for the concert and theatre arts was given high priority by Brigham Young, who continued to act in the new theater.

A former West Point bandmaster, Domenico Ballo, arrived in Salt Lake City and soon launched not only a band but a church orchestra which consisted of a violin, trumpet, flute, cello, and clarinet. Ballo also directed his musicians for dramatic performances and other events in the Social Hall.

Even without an organ, the Choir, performing only twice each year, greatly impressed a French botanist, Jules Remy, and his companion, Julius Brenchley. The two spent a month in Salt Lake City in 1855 and published *A Journey to Great Salt Lake City* in 1861. Remy and Brenchley described the October General Conference:

> At each meeting, the religious exercises began as soon as the president announced that the business of the day was to begin. Then the choristers and band belonging to the choir executed a piece of one of our greatest masters; and we feel bound to say that the Mormons have a feeling for sacred music, that their women sing with soul, and that the execution is in no notable degree surpassed by that which is heard either under the roof of Westminster, or the frescoes of the Sistine chapel.

The pioneers had come west for the express purpose of founding a new Zion, a Kingdom of God on Earth. In the religion of the Saints, grounded in the teachings of a *Book of Mormon* prophet who said, "Man is, that he might have joy," music and the arts still held a hallowed place.

Five conductors guided the Choir through its infancy, a period of two decades which ended with the completion of the new Tabernacle. They served comparatively short terms, from two to five years each. The youngest was thirty, the oldest, sixty years of age when they were chosen to direct the Choir. All served

The Salt Lake Theatre

without remuneration, but with distinction, in these important, formative years. At the same time, each was finding other ways to support his family, establish a home, and further contribute to the cultural life of the community in other fields, including the theater.

Only one was a native-born American, the remaining four having come from Great Britain: one from North Wales, one from Ireland, and two from England. Only one, Charles John Thomas, had made a professional career of his music. He and two others were instrumental, rather than vocal, musicians. And only one, Stephen H. Goddard, had acquired a reputation as a vocalist.

The Choir was small by its own modern standards, but well suited to the size of the early structures in which it sang. When larger vocal forces were needed, two or more prominent choirs from individual wards in the Territory were selected to participate with the permanent Choir. At least two men who were eventually to become Tabernacle Choir conductors, Charles Thomas and Evan Stephens, may have come to the attention of Church leaders as the directors of local choirs participating in General Conference.

The first pipe organ arrived during this period, having crossed the Pacific Ocean from Australia, and the first Tabernacle organist, then eleven, arrived soon after from across the Atlantic. A new, significant era of growth was about to open for the Tabernacle Choir.

John Parry, the first conductor of the Choir, was born in Newmarket, Flintshire, North Wales, on February 10, 1789. Of his early life and musical training before his journey to Salt Lake City, little is known. He arrived in Salt Lake City in 1849 during his sixtieth year and was soon appointed conductor of the Choir —probably by Brigham Young. He served from 1849 to 1854, during which time his Choir performed in the second Bowery and in the adobe Tabernacle. A call to return to Great Britain as a missionary ended his service to the Choir.

Succeeding Parry was a native of New York State, Stephen H. Goddard, then forty-four years old. In Nauvoo, he had been a warden of the School of Music at Nauvoo University and a member of the Nauvoo police department. A noted singer, he was with the original group of pioneers in 1847. He directed the Choir from 1854 to 1856 during the General Conferences of the period. It was one of these occasions which made such a favorable impression on the French botanist and his friend.

James Smithies was a widely known English convert to the Church who had been acquainted with Brigham Young since 1840. Then an Apostle, Young was directing missionary work in the British Isles when they met at a British General Conference, at which William Clayton served as clerk. After immigrating to Nauvoo, he joined the Nauvoo Band and, along with Clayton and Pitt, performed musical selections at the Nauvoo Temple. He was forty-six at the time of his appointment, and served six years, the longest term among the early conductors. During this time, Joseph Ridges's pipe organ arrived and was installed in the Old Tabernacle. An early newspaper account of General Conference records the presence of the organ and reports an important innovation which presaged later

Choir developments—the invitation to other choirs to participate at the General Conference. The *Deseret News* reported:

> Besides the usual choir led by Brother James Smithies, which sits at the south and where the organ is situated, there were today two additional choirs. The 14th Ward choir led by Brother Charles Thomas was near the entrance to the stand and the third choir led by Brother David O. Calder was seated on the west of the stand. These choirs sang alternately.

The choral music development of Salt Lake City had produced three choirs considered capable of performing at Conference. The idea of combining several small choirs was soon to follow, leading eventually to a permanent large Choir for the Tabernacle.

Charles John Thomas, whose choir sang in the General Conference with Smithies's and Calder's, became the Choir's fourth director in 1862, at the age of thirty. He was the first to have made a career in professional music. At nine, he was performing on the violin with his father in a professional orchestra in Newcastle-on-Tyne, before moving to London to continue his musical training. He also composed many pieces which were performed on the London stage. He was twenty-eight when he immigrated to the United States in 1860, and after a brief sojourn in New York, he walked from the Mississippi to Salt Lake City.

Brigham Young soon appointed Thomas as the head and musical director of his favorite artistic venture, the Salt Lake Theatre, the best such facility between Chicago and San Francisco. (In the nineteenth century, most plays were accompanied by incidental music which served the same function as movie music today.) Very little printed music was available, so C. J. Thomas composed his own scores for the small volunteer orchestra, solo singers, and chorus.

Thomas was soon called to be the conductor of the Choir as well. For the dedication of the theater he composed and conducted an *Ode to Brigham Young* for choir and orchestra. At the ceremony, Brigham presented a definitive statement of Mormon esthetics:

> Everything that is joyful, beautiful, glorious, comforting, consoling, lovely, pleasing to the eye, good to the taste, pleasant to the smell, and happifying in every respect is for the Saints.
>
> Tight-laced religious professors of the present generation have a horror at the sound of a fiddle. There is no music in hell, for all good music belongs to heaven. Sweet harmonious sounds give exquisite joy to human beings capable of appreciating music. I delight in hearing harmonious tones made by the human voice, by musical instruments, and by both combined. Every sweet musical sound that can be made belongs to the Saints and is for the Saints. Every flower, shrub and tree to beautify, and to gratify the taste and smell, and every sensation that gives to man joy and felicity are for the Saints who receive them from the Most High.

Thomas would yield the Choir podium before the new Tabernacle was occupied. The conductor who moved the Choir from the Old Tabernacle to its new home was an Irishman, Robert Sands. He was thirty-seven at the time, and served for four years, before being succeeded by the first of the truly accomplished Mormon conductors to follow—each one placing his stamp more permanently on the Choir than any of their predecessors. But Sands would see Joseph J. Daynes begin his thirty-three years as the first Tabernacle organist, starting on the imported pipe organ in the adobe building and continuing on the instrument he would help build and on which he was to perform until the turn of the century.

4

And Organs

A BOY'S FASCINATION with an organ-factory "fairy land" near London, a prospector's passion for gold in Australia and America, an organ shipped halfway around the world in soldered tin boxes, a threat to destroy a wagon train, hiding an organ from the U.S. Army, a great choir's need for a worthy instrument, a very large musical talent packaged, initially, in a very small boy: these ingredients open the improbable saga of a musical instrument of unique character which would evolve for a century as its sounds and its image became world-famed.

Born in England, Joseph Harris Ridges was twenty-four when he took his family to Australia to prospect for gold. On board ship he met several Latter-day Saints, and the Ridges family eventually converted to Mormonism. After a time in the backcountry, he settled his family in Sydney and worked as a carpenter. He later recalled: "Having a little money coming to me I began to build my first organ, which by the way was the first organ to be built in Australia. I had plenty of time on my hands and I worked night and day at the instrument."

Ridges had first become fascinated by organs as a boy, when he lived across the street from an organ factory: "I used to sometimes pass beyond those gates and revel in the mysteries of that organ factory and watch the men at their work, and study and think out the purposes and uses of the numerous things the mechanics were at work upon."

The first organ Ridges built didn't remain in Australia. The Church needed it in Utah, so the Ridges family disassembled the instrument, packaged the parts in soldered tin shipping cases, and took sail.

In 1856, the schooner *Jenny Lind* took them all to San Pedro, California. Joseph Ridges stayed for the winter in Los Angeles, while the organ was shipped ahead to the Mormon colony in San Bernadino. The presiding elder from Australia had meanwhile arrived in Salt Lake City and spoken to Brigham Young about the organ. Brigham sent word that the instrument was to be brought to Salt Lake. So, in the spring of 1857, twelve wagons pulled by fourteen mule teams left San Bernadino headed east. In that year, the colony had encountered real difficulties with its neighbors, and its population had been threatened with violence. It is testimony to the Mormons' concern for music that, in the midst of an imperiled colony and real physical danger, a group of people took the time to transport and protect such unwieldy and "nonfunctional" cargo.

On October 11, 1857, the organ was played for the first time during a regular Choir rehearsal at the old adobe Tabernacle, which was intended to be its home for the next ten years.

But the organ was soon moved again. In 1858, after President James Buchanan had been told the Mormons were in "a state of revolt," the United States government sent a contingent of troops to help establish federal control in the Utah territories. When the troops arrived they found that the Mormons had abandoned the city and moved about fifty miles south to Provo, leaving vacant homes and empty warehouses. Straw was packed against every building, ready for the torch. The settlers had deserted their homes, but they had taken the organ south with them, considering it valuable enough to save even though they had to disassemble the complex machine in a very short time.

A compromise was reached—the troops remained stationed outside of Salt Lake City but Brigham was allowed to retain effective power over the territorial government—and the organ soon returned to its home in the Old Tabernacle. (When the Old Tabernacle was finally replaced, much of Joseph Ridges's first organ eventually found new purpose in the Assembly Hall constructed on the Old Tabernacle site. Some of the pipes remain in use to this day, after 120 years on Temple Square.)

As the New Tabernacle was in the process of being built, Brigham Young asked Ridges if he could construct a new, larger organ to accompany the Choir in its new home. "I told him that I thought it could be done—whereupon he asked me to draw preliminary plans," Ridges recalled later. Having built one organ, he was now ready for his masterpiece.

After securing authorization to go ahead, Ridges hired several "skillful and intelligent mechanics," Shure Olsen, Neils Johnson, David Anderson, William Pinney, and John Sandberg, none of whom had ever worked on an organ. Later, Frank Woods, who knew something of the art, joined the team.

Ridges traveled to Boston to purchase the parts which could not be made at home. In Boston, he probably saw the Boston Hall organ (built in 1863 and since reinstalled in the Methuen Memorial Hall), which the wooden case of the Tabernacle organ strongly resembles, including identical angels at the top. The really amazing thing is that the artisans of Utah were able to equal an instrument created by the most experienced and well-equipped craftsmen of the East.

Brigham Young sent scouts to bring back wood samples for the Tabernacle organ, of which the great pines of Washington County met with Ridges's approval: their wood was straight, knot-free, and without pitch or gum. But Wash-

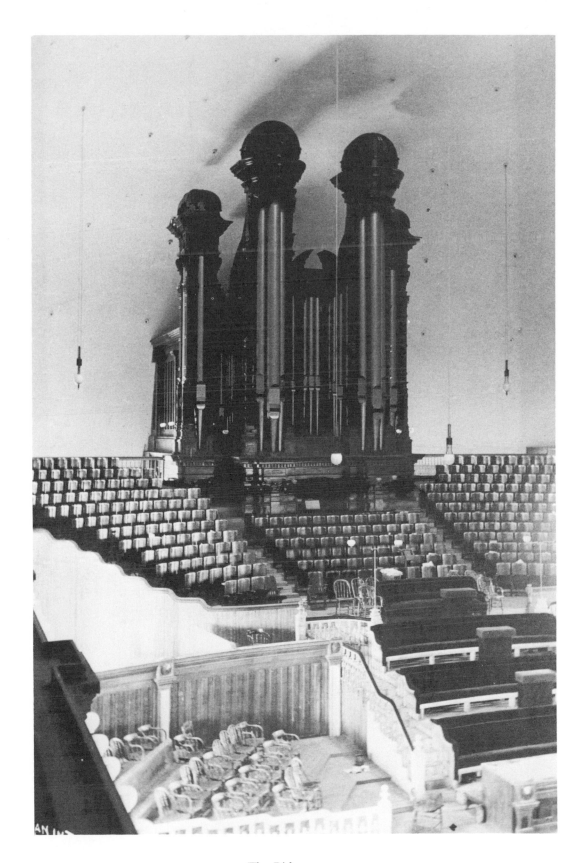

The Ridges organ

Joseph J. Daynes

ington County was some 300 miles from Salt Lake City, and a great many of these miles were in Indian territory.

Nevertheless, lumber was brought to Salt Lake City, and Ridges and his crew began construction in January 1866. As the organ was being built, the concept of what it should be grew grander. The organ's visible "signature" is the round thirty-two-foot gilded pipes, the most striking features of the façade. They are the world's only round wooden pipes of this size and are made of laminated wedge-shaped pieces of wood which were fitted together to form the cylindrical shape. The pipes are lined with canvas glued to the inside. It is still a mystery how this was done. The explanation proposed by a former technician at the Tabernacle is that perhaps the pipes were made on the keystone principle, with the cloth being glued in place before the last strip was placed into its slot. The organ also employed a system of bellows, which four men pumped to provide sufficient air pressure. (A direct-current motor was installed in 1898.)

The organ was first played publicly on October 6, 1867, for the thirty-seventh semi-annual General Conference. Although Ridges's crew had been unable to have it properly tuned, "it was . . . ," according to the *Deseret News,* "in a condition to accompany the Choir and Brigham was pleased with it."

Ridges never lost the prospecting bug which had originally taken him to Australia, and whenever it was rumored that gold had been found somewhere in Utah, off he would go, leaving glue, wood, and metal behind. Brigham, remarkably tolerant, would simply dispatch some of his men to find Professor Ridges and bring him back home. Ridges's associate Neils Johnson eventually took over for him and brought the organ to its initial stage of completion, making it into a truly functional instrument.

It is one thing to build a great organ, and quite another to perform on it. Neither Ridges nor any of his "skillful and intelligent mechanics" was an organist. Five years after Ridges's original organ was installed in the old adobe Tabernacle, a boy and his family arrived in Salt Lake City from their native England. As legend has it, the boy was welcomed by Brigham Young with the words, "There is the organist for our great Tabernacle organ."

The youth had already demonstrated unusual talent. The son of an amateur musician in Norwich, England, Joseph J. Daynes was playing the piano at the age of two and, before emigrating, capped a promising concert career with an organ recital performed in the presence of Queen Victoria—at the tender age of eleven.

Crossing the plains, the family's ox-pulled wagon contained their most important possessions, an old harmonium and Joseph's concertina, which earned him many invitations to sit alongside the wagon drivers. At night, father John Daynes led the singing, with harmonium accompaniment by his son.

When he sat at Ridges's first organ, Joseph's legs would not reach the pedals until blocks of cork were added to the soles of his shoes. Although still little more than a child, he also maintained and tuned the instrument, a difficult task whenever temperatures inside a building vary sharply, as they did in these structures. Young Daynes was then appointed by Brigham Young as advisor to Ridges on

The building of the New Tabernacle. The two men standing on the stone pillars (front and center) give a sense of the enormous size of the building.

The Salt Lake Temple under construction, with the old Tabernacle, left, and the new Tabernacle, right, in the background.

the construction of his new organ. And when the great organ was dedicated and first played, Joseph Daynes was at the console; he was fifteen years old.

Daynes was Tabernacle organist for thirty-three years and accompanied the Choir at rehearsals and performances. For rehearsals, he played on a small harmonium which, in the earlier days of the Choir, provided more than enough sound.

One day Daynes sat down to perform at a recital, but the organ was silent. He checked his stops and combinations and began again. Nothing. He ran backstage to find his four bellows-pumpers sitting down on the job. "We feel that it is unfair that you get all the credit for these recitals," said one of the group. "Without us, there wouldn't be any recital. We want to be recognized too!" Gallantly, Joseph Daynes brought out the four bellows-men, introducing each by name to the audience. They then returned to their pumps and the recital went on as scheduled.

Daynes made his living as a teacher, producing many of Utah's finest organists. His work at Temple Square was on a purely voluntary basis, though he received occasional money from his playing at the Tabernacle; the Church contributed money for special events or recitals, or the hat was passed and recital audiences would contribute.

By the early 1860s, Salt Lake City was no longer a lonely outpost. The 1849 Gold Rush, the Pony Express, the Oregon Trail, the stagecoach, and the settlement of an empire stretching from Canada to Mexico had changed all that. And two years after the Tabernacle's completion, the east and west legs of the transcontinental railroad would be joined at a spot some eighty miles northwest of Temple Square, and the Mormon capital would truly become the "Crossroads of the West."

Three times in twenty years, the Salt Lake City Mormons had outgrown their central meeting place. When they built the fourth time, the Salt Lake Tabernacle was planned on a visionary scale to last a century, and more. Temple Square was the scene of almost frenetic activity. On the east side of the block, the Salt Lake Temple was slowly rising, granite block by granite block, from the deep excavation in which its foundations were embedded. The subterranean works, hastily covered over with mounds of dirt when the invasion by the U.S. Army appeared imminent in 1858, had been uncovered and construction renewed, requiring shops for masons, stonecutters, and carpenters.

The new Tabernacle was the focus of construction work on the west half of the square, its elaborate scaffolding rising both inside and outside the oval of forty-four red sandstone buttresses. The building's twenty-eight doors would be hung between them, and the gigantic arched roof would rest on them entirely without central support. Work had already proceeded on the Tabernacle for four years before Ridges and his organ builders set up shop alongside.

The building of the Tabernacle from 1863 to 1867 was a marvelous accomplishment of design, construction, and utility. A triumvirate of architects designed the building; William H. Folsom created the exterior, Henry Grow built

Eliza Snow

the roof, and Truman O. Angell executed the interior, eventually becoming a member of the Choir in the Tabernacle which he designed.

Grow had been a bridge engineer and he hit upon the happy idea of building the Tabernacle roof in a consecutive series of arch-bridges. Two rows of stone pillars were placed a hundred and fifty feet apart and spanned with latticed wooden arches. Arch pieces, each twelve or fourteen feet long, twelve inches wide, and two or three inches thick, were connected together at the joints with 1¼-inch wooden dowels covered with glue and driven into round holes. If the wood split, builders bound the adjacent pieces with wet rawhide. When dry, the rawhide bonds were immovable. The original plaster, which still lines the inside of the Tabernacle shell, is so thick that horsehair was used as a binder. Very few nails were used in the construction of the Tabernacle, since transportation through hundreds of miles of hostile territory made their cost exorbitant.

Seats for the Choir were at the west end of the new Tabernacle, in front of the towering pipes of the new organ, but were not yet arranged in the steep, amphitheatric pattern so familiar today. The Choir was on the same elevation as the audience but placed inside the railing which surrounded the small speaker's stand.

At the inaugural General Conference, there were still no permanent seats, the horseshoe-shaped balcony was not installed, and there was no lighting or heating. Among several hymns the Choir sang during the Conference was "Praise, Praise, O Praise the Great I Am!" by Eliza R. Snow, one of the greatest LDS hymn writers, composed especially for the occasion. She also wrote one of the most beloved of Mormon hymns, "O My Father," a poem which has been set to music by several composers.

Recognizing that the Conference and Tabernacle were not just for the people of Salt Lake City, choirs from all over Deseret were invited to sing. The choirs of Springville, Spanish Fork, and Payson combined to form one ensemble; singers from Brigham City and Smithfield made up another. Brass bands from Ogden and Nephi performed after the Conference sessions on the grounds of Temple Square.

As if by design, all the necessary elements—except one—for a new era of music among the Mormons came together in 1867: the arts enjoyed the continued encouragement of Brigham Young, a growing population provided an adequate supply of vocal talent, the Choir and the great organ were in their new, permanent home, and a remarkably accomplished, if youthful, organist was already serving. It was a time of new opportunities, lacking only a musical director equal to the task. Two years later, the final ingredient was added.

George Edward Percy Careless

5

Mission

Brigham Young stood up and said, "Brother George, I have a mission for you. I want you to take the Tabernacle Choir and the theater orchestra and lay a foundation for good music in Utah." George Careless accepted the call.

The message was familiar in style and delivery. Brigham Young was accustomed to issuing mission calls. Without warning or consultation, Latter-day Saints were told where they were needed: a proselyting mission in Europe or the southern states, a colonizing assignment in Idaho or Mexico.

But this welcome summons was different. It made good music an ecclesiastical as well as social objective, a religious as well as aesthetic assignment. It may explain the zeal with which the call was fulfilled.

George Careless was born in London on September 24, 1839, and displayed musical talent early in life—much to the consternation of his father, a woodcarver, who told him he should not waste his time with music but should learn a useful trade. George dutifully apprenticed with a shoemaking company. The plant foreman, however, was a music lover who collected violins. He told George to think of nothing but music for a career and loaned him a violin.

George learned to play the fiddle and also was an accomplished boy soprano. At the age of ten, he was offered a place in a London choir school (where boys earned their academic and musical education by singing in a church or cathedral choir), but turned it down. He was a recent convert to The Church of Jesus Christ of Latter-day Saints. Then George's father presented an ultimatum: give up music or leave the family. When he was thirteen, George left home for good.

The shoe-factory foreman, a Mr. Ross, loaned young Careless the money to attend the Royal Academy, Britain's premier music school, a debt George was to repay from professional earnings. Mr. Ross was a man of either keen judgment or great faith. George finished in three years instead of the usual four, studying violin, piano, conducting, voice, and musical theory.

Saints Leaving Liverpool by Ken Baxter depicts the common scene of Mormon emigrant vessels departing for New York.

This was an optimistic age for England, and the English built a glittering structure of glass, a Crystal Palace, to display their accomplishments. The orchestra which presented concerts there was itself a triumph of the empire. There were 256 violinists in the ensemble and a total of 1,200 musicians in all. George Careless was engaged to be a member of the orchestra. It was a good experience for him, once he became acquainted with a varied repertoire and observed at first hand the methods used to administer a large performing body. Careless also devoted a great deal of energy to the musical activities of the English LDS Church, directing a London Conference Choir until it became so proficient that it was invited to perform at several of London's leading concert halls.

George's career was developing handsomely when Elder William C. Staines encouraged him to move to Salt Lake City. Staines realized that if George stayed in London, he might not be willing to sacrifice fame and fortune to emigrate. Six weeks later, George sailed for America.

Like so many Mormon immigrant vessels, his became a ship of song as the Saints sang hymns of hope and praise, and George Careless led the choir. The Mormons felt that their religion was the realization of the prophecy of Isaiah: "And it shall come to pass in the last days, that the mountain of the Lord's house shall be established in the top of the mountains, and shall be exalted above the hills; and all nations shall flow unto it."

The *Hudson* docked in New York City July 19, 1864. Its captain, impressed by the singing of his passengers, asked Careless for "one of his tunes" that he might sing it with his family on Sunday evenings. Careless's sheet music was already packed away, so he simply sat down at a bacon barrel and wrote a song, which he called "Hudson," in the ship's honor. Assembling his choir, Careless performed it for the thankful captain. Parley P. Pratt's poem, "The Morning Breaks" is set to the "Hudson" tune; it is one of the Church's most beloved hymns.

George Careless, the sophisticated young musician from London, walked from New York to Utah. His arrival in Salt Lake City elicited mixed reactions from another London friend who had preceded him. There were already three professional musicians in the valley, he said, and they were unable to make a living. Careless answered, "I'll stay with my music for two years—if I starve, you will have to bury me."

Within a month George Careless had twenty-four "paying" pupils; the going rate for a series of lessons was a hundred pounds of flour.

It was George Careless's successful classes which attracted Brigham Young's attention. When President Young called Careless to his musical mission, the latter responded: "I will do the best I can with the material I can get." Brigham replied: "You will have to make that."

It was a tough assignment. Careless took charge of the Salt Lake Theatre's volunteer orchestra of sixteen men, who were filled with spirit but not necessarily with any great musical talent. Determined to build a disciplined, reliable ensemble, he decided to pay his musicians. He hired seven men for his orchestra and dismissed the volunteers, causing a dispute which had to be resolved by Brigham

The Salt Lake Theatre Orchestra

Young himself, who agreed with Careless. The new players earned the rather extravagant sum of three dollars a night, in cash. (George Careless's career in the Theatre would come to an untimely and ironical end in the 1870s when his paid musicians joined a "musical union." Professor Careless refused to become a member and was forced to resign from the orchestra.)

Although the programs at the Salt Lake Theatre did not identify the chorus as members of the Tabernacle Choir, Careless had been music director of both, and it is safe to assume that many members of the Choir occasionally wore greasepaint.

The Tabernacle Choir was in no better shape than the theater orchestra had been when Professor Careless took them both over. Careless found only forty members present when he went to his first rehearsal at the Tabernacle. It was a terribly cold night with knee-deep snow, and the Tabernacle was neither heated nor lighted. Singers held a candle in one hand and the music in the other. Professor Careless was not amused. He told Squire Wells, the associate of Brigham Young who had accompanied him to the rehearsal, that he needed at least seventy-five voices for a proper choir, plus an oil-lamp chandelier and a stove. Brother Wells demurred, saying that the improvements would be costly. "Is not the health of the singers of more value than a stove pipe?" asked Professor Careless. By the next week, all his requests had been fulfilled.

Under their talented new director, the Tabernacle Choir flourished. In 1870, one year after his appointment, the *Deseret News* reported:

> The singing during Conference has elicited general and well-merited praise and commendation; and never before, we think, has the Tabernacle Choir been in such a state of efficiency, and the highest credit is due Professor Careless, the conductor, and to the brethren and sisters of the choir for their excellent rendering of the various compositions sung. The anthems "Sanctus," "The Earth Is the Lord's," "How Beautiful upon the Mountains," "Jerusalem, My Glorious Home," sung at various times were excellently rendered, and would have done no discredit to the same number of professional vocalists.

Careless had the quality which, perhaps even more than musicianship, was the necessary attribute of the men who built music in Zion: he was a superb organizer. On October 8, 1873, the Saints heard the first truly substantial "Mormon Tabernacle Choir" at General Conference. This Choir deserves an honored place in Zion's musical history. There were eighty-five people from the Salt Lake Tabernacle Choir and smaller groups from Ogden, Brigham City, Farmington, North Ogden, American Fork, West Jordan, Parowan, Coalville, Willard City (conducted by young Evan Stephens), Logan, Fort Herriman, Wellsville, Spanish Fork, and Bountiful—a total of 304 singers in all.

Organizing such a performance was a major undertaking. Some of these communities were several days' journey from Salt Lake City and transportation was rough and perilous. Reprints of *Sacred Hymns and Spiritual Songs,* the hymnbook which Brigham Young and others had edited in England, were commonly used but still contained no music, and the poems were still sung to a variety of tunes. Careless was confronted with the task of teaching 300 singers a new group of hymn tunes by rote. The texts were all familiar, but sung by the different choirs to different tunes. Careless's first-hand experience with musical chaos undoubtedly led him to consider the need for an official Church-wide hymnbook—with uniform musical settings—and he would have an important role in producing such a work.

For Brigham Young's funeral in 1877, Careless assembled a 220-voice choir to perform a funeral hymn he composed for the occasion, and conducted the orchestra in "Brigham Young's Funeral March," composed by organist Joseph J. Daynes.

Careless resigned in 1880, after eleven years as director of the Tabernacle Choir, but his musical mission continued for many years. In 1875 he directed his Philharmonic Society orchestra and the nonsectarian Handel and Haydn Society's choir in the first performance of Handel's *Messiah* anywhere between Chicago and San Francisco, and he followed in later years with such works as Rossini's *Stabat Mater* and Mendelssohn's *Hymn of Praise.* When Careless first performed the *Messiah,* he was the only person in the entire production who had ever heard the work before.

Brigham Young's successor, President John Taylor, asked Careless to chair a committee of five to write music for all the hymns to be included in *The Latter-day Saints' Psalmody,* published in 1889. Other committee members were his two successors as Choir director, Ebenezer Beesley and Evan Stephens, along with Tabernacle organist Joseph J. Daynes and Thomas C. Griggs, who was originally chosen to succeed Careless, but instead became assistant conductor to Beesley. The *Psalmody* included 330 hymns, three-fourths of them set to music by Mormon composers.

Brigham Young had charged Careless with a mission "to lay a foundation for good music in Utah." Historian Edward Tullidge observed, "In Professor Careless's career in Salt Lake City may be traced the germination of musical taste in our city."

If the mission of George Careless was to build a foundation for good music, it was Ebenezer Beesley who preserved it from destruction.

The last of the British-trained musicians to direct the Tabernacle Choir, Beesley pushed and pulled a handcart across the plains, his bride at his side, still wearing her wedding dress. The rickety vehicle not only held his instruments and their other worldly belongings, but also carried a woman the young couple befriended who was too feeble to make the journey on foot. This same kindness toward others in times of hardship marked Beesley's years directing the Choir, which came as the powerful forces of the United States Congress were directed against the Church's practice of plural marriage, or polygamy. Beesley's ascension to the directorship was a classic case of the understudy doing so well that he becomes the star.

Ebenezer Beesley, the sixth of seven choir directors born in Great Britain, was a native of Bicester, Oxfordshire. When he was only two years old, he was observed singing along with adults who made the Beesley home their choir rehearsal hall. At the age of nine, he became a Mormon, along with others of his family. Before they emigrated from England, he had mastered both the violin and the flute. He thus imported his musical qualifications to Zion as had the five other British Choir directors before him.

The handcart with which the young Beesleys made the long journey across mid-America was one of thousands built in Nebraska and Iowa by the Mormons themselves. The Eighth Handcart Company included 235 people and sixty handcarts under the direction of Captain George Rowley. Ebenezer Beesley led them in song on the trail by day and around the campfire with his flute by night. By all accounts, "The Handcart Song" was the favorite of the trip. In part it goes:

> *Ye Saints that dwell on Europe's shores,*
> *Prepare yourselves with many more*
> *To leave behind your native land*
> > *For sure God's Judgments are at hand.*
> *Prepare to cross the stormy main*
> *Before you do the valley gain*
> *And with the faithful make a start*
> > *To cross the plains with your handcart.*

REFRAIN:

> *Some must push and some must pull*
> > *As we go marching up the hill,*
> *As merrily on the way we go*
> > *Until we reach the valley, oh.*

The members of the company were soon to have less to sing about. The terrain was hard, and fatigue was a constant enemy. Indians harried them along the route. The company was a twenty-five-day walk from Salt Lake City when the last of their food gave out. When Brigham Young learned of the company's plight he sent supply trains laden with food. Their spirits revived, they once again made music. Apostle John Taylor had come with the relief train. Later, as President of the Church, he would call Beesley to service with the Choir. Taylor wrote, "Some of the young people were very joyous and jubilant. There were among them many beautiful singers, who entertained us in the evening, around their campfires, with some of the late popular airs, and among the rest several amusing handcart songs."

A band had come up to Emigration Canyon to escort the company on its way to the city. When Beesley heard a man playing on a tin whistle, he said to his wife, "If that man can play a tune on a tin whistle, he can play a flute."

Beesley followed in his father's trade when he first arrived in Salt Lake,

---

45

Ebenezer Beesley

working as a shoemaker. He quickly became the director of his ward choir and director of music at the ward Sunday School, which, in the LDS Church, has classes for people of all ages, not just children. Beesley soon was invited to join Dimick Huntington's Martial Band, a group of self-taught musicians whose lack of musical skills enabled them only to play the same melody in unison, though probably not all in the same key at the same time. Beesley taught them to read music, and, what was possibly more important to their listeners, to play in harmony. He eventually became the band's leader. The Huntington Band has the somewhat dubious honor of being the only ensemble ever to give a concert playing from the roof of the Salt Lake Tabernacle.

Beesley was also the leader of the Salt Lake Theatre's volunteer orchestra and was hired as one of the musicians when George Careless made it a professional orchestra. Professor Beesley continued to perform with this ensemble until shortly before his death.

In 1880, Beesley was selected to become the assistant director of the Choir. George Careless had resigned as director and Thomas C. Griggs, named as his replacement, was at that time on a mission in Europe. Beesley was asked to fill in. When Griggs returned, he didn't want to "disturb the present successful management of the Choir" and offered to become Beesley's assistant. The newspapers reported that "the proposal was carried without dissent, the best of feeling prevailing."

While past Tabernacle Choirs had little continuity and were assembled for rehearsals only in anticipation of General Conference or some other special event, the Choir had by this time become a group of singers with a strong identification with each other, and their new director nurtured this growing sense of fraternity.

Aside from the opportunity to develop one's vocal talents, the primary motivation for most of those who joined the Tabernacle Choir was religious service. Ebenezer Beesley is credited with making it, in addition, a social and even recreational association, and this during some of the darkest days of Utah's history.

The Choir members believed in helping their own in times of adversity. On November 9, 1883, the Choir unanimously passed a resolution stating:

FIRST. That a perpetual benefit fund be maintained by the Tabernacle Choir.

SECOND. That all proceeds from any source, the results of the efforts of the Choir, in giving concerts or parties, etc., or from donation, belong to the said fund.

THIRD. That no individual member has any right to use the monies belonging to said fund for any purpose whatever, without first obtaining the permission of a majority vote of the members of the Choir present at any regular meeting.

FOURTH. That said funds may be used for any purpose whatever that a majority of the members of the Choir present at any regular meeting may decide upon.

Choir members and Church officials jailed for polygamy in the Utah Territorial
Penitentiary in the late 1800s.

FIFTH. That any person, in order to become entitled to the benefits of said fund, must have been a faithful member of the Choir for at least six months. That this be considered the rule, unless any time it shall be suspended, by a majority vote of the Choir members.

They also discussed the advantages of presenting many concerts, both to achieve musical excellence and assure financial independence.

The Choir spent its money with great sensitivity. "It was unanimously decided to donate the sum of Twenty-five Dollars from the Choir funds to assist Brother Jos. Bentley to defray the expenses he has had to meet in the untimely death of his aged Brother, who strayed from his residence and died of exposure to the cold." Widows of Choir members received support, as did accident victims and people whose farms had been destroyed by fire.

Brother William H. Foster, a respected member (and, in fact, the oldest member of the Choir) having recently met with a sad bereavement, in the death of his oldest son, a youth of 26 years, after but a brief illness, leaving a wife and two young children—it was moved and seconded, and unanimously agreed, that the Tabernacle express its regrets and sympathy by a donation of Twenty-five Dollars from its Fund, to assist in providing a house and home for the widow and fatherless children.

When the Choir traveled from Salt Lake City to American Fork, Utah, on an "excursion" in 1880, the event bore more of the trappings of a picnic than a concert appearance. The festivities began with an overture by a group of singer-instrumentalists called the Tabernacle Orchestral Band under Professor Beesley's direction. Professor Daynes "executed a polka on the organ, with imitations of various musical instruments." Capping the festivities was an afternoon of dancing.

The period of heady accomplishment begun during the life of President Brigham Young was brought abruptly to an end in the 1880s as Congress took determined steps to stop the practice of polygamy among the Mormons. The conflict had severe ramifications for the community, and for the Choir.

The Civil War and Reconstruction had delayed the government's antipolygamy campaign, but by the late 1800s, Congress had turned again to the "Mormon Question." The Edmunds Act of 1882 made polygamy a felony, and polygamists were disenfranchised. The Mormons challenged the Act in the courts, but the Supreme Court declared the disenfranchisement provisions constitutional.

Federal authorities enforced the law by wholesale arrests. In a classic act of passive civil disobedience, many Mormons went underground. Others spent up to two and a half years in the Utah penitentiary. Utah's attempts to gain statehood were doomed to fail so long as the polygamy issue remained unsettled.

In 1887, the amended Edmunds-Tucker Act declared the Church itself disincorporated. The Church was required to forfeit all property valued at more than $50,000, although it was allowed to use its property (including Temple Square) on a rental basis. The Church took its case once again to the Supreme Court and again lost. In 1890, the Court upheld the provisions of the Edmunds-Tucker Act which had dissolved the Mormon Church.

Choir attendance, particularly in the men's sections, was decimated by the federal prosecutions. With many in jail, and others in hiding, Beesley faced difficult times with a kindly patience and grace which endeared him to all. The Choir attempted to help its members who were in jail "for conscience sake," with Thomas Griggs administering a fund to help support their families.

On September 24, 1890, with the concurrence of his two counselors and the Council of the Twelve, Wilford Woodruff, Taylor's successor as President of the Church, issued a statement: "I publicly declare that my advice to the Latter-day Saints is to refrain from conducting any marriage forbidden by the law of the land." The Manifesto, as this statement became known, was unanimously approved by the next General Conference. Polygamy within the Church was officially ended and the road to eventual statehood for Utah opened.

Through this troubled decade, under Beesley's direction, the Choir sang, going on excursions and keeping a semblance of order. It was a rare accomplishment. Wrote Church President John Taylor to Beesley: "I take pleasure in saying to you that I am highly gratified with the manner in which you have conducted the Tabernacle Choir since you have had charge thereof . . . in the unanimity of feelings which seems to exist among the members . . . in the excellent execution and rendition of both vocal and instrumental part." It was a sentiment shared by many in the community.

Beesley was a quiet, gentle man especially delighting in the company of children (he had twelve of his own by his two wives) and he took genuine pride in the hymns which he had composed for young people. An active composer, he wrote many anthems and hymns, several of which are still in regular use, and published *A Collection of Hymns and Anthems: set to music by home composers for the use of the Salt Lake Tabernacle Choir*, in the *Juvenile Instructor,* a youth magazine, in 1883. It preceded the *Latter-day Saints' Psalmody,* setting the tone for that book. The pieces were composed with a choir in mind, uniquely emphasizing it (as opposed to the congregation) as the performing medium for ordinary Church usage. The Tabernacle Choir was a major influence on this mode of expression.

Ebenezer Beesley retired from his directorship of the Choir in 1889, to be·succeeded by Evan Stephens. Beesley moved to Lehi, Utah, and assumed command of the Lehi Choir, which he led to victory at a state choir festival that same year.

6

Hosanna

To TWELVE-YEAR-OLD EVAN STEPHENS, everything in life was an adventure—especially the thousand-mile walk across the Great Plains: "I don't know whether the pioneers enjoyed it. The journey across the plains was such an experience of pleasure to me, that I found it difficult to sympathize with the pioneers who found it a hardship. I was too elated to walk so I would run ahead, and then I would stop and wait for the crowd."

And he was to run for the rest of his life, his energy increasing as he grew older.

Stephens was born on June 28, 1854, in Pencader, Carmarthenshire, South Wales. His parents had been converted to The Church of Jesus Christ of Latter-day Saints by Captain Dan Jones, a Welshman who became a Mississippi riverboat captain, bringing Mormon immigrants up the river from New Orleans to Nauvoo.

Jones returned to his homeland as a missionary during the "hungry forties," a low ebb in the history of that proud land. Through their belief in the prophecies of Joseph Smith, the Mormons could speak of the United States as a Zion in religious as well as economic terms—a place where men could be free to work, and free to be saved. Within twenty years of Dan Jones's first mission, more than twenty percent of all foreign immigrants coming to Utah were from Wales—and many were fine singers.

The Stephens family had lived in extreme poverty in Wales. Evan was forced to quit school at an early age to help support the family. When they arrived in Utah in 1866, they spent only a week in Salt Lake City before joining other relatives in Willard, a small town fifty miles to the north. The Welsh boy worked hard at what jobs he could find, herding sheep and cattle (the only skill he knew) and hauling lumber. Having grown up speaking Welsh, Evan spent his evenings learning English.

There was a good church choir in Willard, led by David Tobey, a Welshman,

The Choir of the 15th Ward, Salt Lake City, typified the small choral groups in
local Mormon congregations.

and since Evan wanted to learn music, he joined, singing with the altos.

Even at this early age, Stephens displayed remarkable tenacity and single-mindedness, devoting his every spare moment to music. In a year with the choir he learned basic musicianship, how to read music and sing, and also acquired the rudiments of accordion, flute, and organ playing. He eventually became the choir's leader.

In the 1870s, George Careless invited other choirs to supplement the 150-member Tabernacle Choir during General Conferences. The Church was striving to develop music throughout Utah, and since the Choir was intended to serve as a model, both in singing style and repertoire, the Conferences gave these smaller choirs an opportunity to hear the preferred style first-hand and to expand their own repertoires. Nevertheless, some members of the Logan and Ogden Tabernacle choirs declared that their respective choirs could beat the pants off the Salt Lakers any day.

Stephens too was invited to bring his Willard Choir to Conference. Although printed music was still scarce and choirs had to learn new pieces by rote, Stephens, on two months' notice, taught his choir twenty-four hymns and anthems —with no sheet music and without a trained musician in the group.

Even as a very young man, Stephens was already the master of a unique kind of inspirational leadership, and it was this ability which colored all of his contributions to Utah's musical life and is why he stands as the giant of early Utah music.

Directing the Willard Choir was volunteer work and Stephens still had to attend to his farm duties, which took up about fifteen hours a day in the summers, and only a few hours less in the winters. His choir sang for two church meetings on Sunday and rehearsed once during the week, with occasional concerts requiring extra rehearsals. Stephens also played the organ for the hymn singing at Sunday School and led the singing at the weekly men's Priesthood meeting In addition, he conducted the town glee club once or twice a week, and taught a music-reading class.

Stephens had taught himself the rudiments of composition, and his first pieces appeared in the pages of the *Juvenile Instructor* in 1873. George Beesley, its editor, regularly published music by "home composers," as Utah musicians were called in that day.

Stephens took leave of his choir in Willard to find adventure working on the railroad. Trains had only recently come to Utah, and after the Golden Spike ceremony at Promontory, Utah, in 1869 had linked the East and West coasts, thousands of workmen were needed to build tracks connecting the major cities of Utah to the railroad. Often the companies were Church-sponsored, since the Mormons were anxious to improve transportation for the converts and settlers who were pouring in from the eastern United States and abroad.

Stephens remained musically active even while working on the railroad, and continued to develop his reputation. In 1879, he was invited to become the organist of the Logan Mormon Tabernacle. With his customary energy, Stephens threw himself into a whirlwind of musical activity. On August 7, 1880, he presented the operetta *The May Queen*—with words and music by Evan Stephens.

This was the first operetta composed and produced in Utah—a completely staged musical theater piece, in one of the smaller cities of the Territory, with entirely home-grown talent.

Stephens loved children and they adored him. Throughout his life he took great pleasure in the company of young people, and was able to bring out their best. In Logan, he organized his first singing classes for children, classes of 100 or more, and presented selections from Gilbert and Sullivan's *H.M.S. Pinafore* in 1880 with 110 children on stage. Since the desire to learn music knew no age barriers in pioneer Utah, popular demand led to an adult class.

In 1882, the Deseret Sunday School Union invited him to organize singing classes for children in Salt Lake City. Within a few months, his class of 250 boys and girls presented a concert in the Salt Lake Theatre. It was a huge success: not only did the box-office proceeds cover the cost of the concert (as rare in those days as it is today), but within a week 400 more children had joined the class. Eventually, Stephens graduated almost 2,000 children each year who could read music and sing.

Stephens's dedication to music education continued throughout his life. He was supervisor of music at both the University of Deseret and the public school system in the Territory and, later, the state. When not teaching, he was composing and studying the organ.

In the nineteen years after his arrival in Utah as an unlearned boy, Evan Stephens had become the most promising musical prodigy of the indigenous Mormon musical culture. In five more years, at the age of thirty-six, he would become the most significant conductor in the annals of the Tabernacle Choir. His musical genius had been shaped entirely by the Mormon musicians, both lay and professional, he had come to know in Utah. His organ teacher was Tabernacle organist Joseph J. Daynes. His compositions—and presumably his conducting—were strongly influenced by George Careless and Ebenezer Beesley.

The immigrant country boy was now thirty-one, unmarried (he remained a bachelor), and still moved by a spirit of adventure. Eager for some serious advanced training in music, especially in composition, Stephens decided to travel to Boston. His first sojourn in the outside world was characterized by a paradoxical mixture of astonishing discovery and frustrating disappointment.

Stephens entered the New England Conservatory, the leading music school in the United States, and was overwhelmed by the musical activity in Boston. There he attended every concert he could find and discovered and fell in love with opera. He spent $150 on printed music which he immediately sent home for future study and use.

Stephens's composition professor at the conservatory was George Whitefield Chadwick, a man already well on his way to becoming one of America's most distinguished teachers and composers. He and Stephens enjoyed a fine working relationship, until Chadwick walked into class drunk one day. The Church's dietary code, the Word of Wisdom, forbids the use of alcohol for anything but medicinal purposes, and, shocked, Stephens returned to Utah, vowing that he could never learn a thing from such a man. The distinguished Utah composer

Leroy Robertson, who studied with Chadwick thirty years later, observed that "Chadwick's drink set Mormon music back fifty years."

It is also possible that Stephens was homesick in Boston; he had written to one of his favorite sopranos back home a rather heartsick song entitled "My Friend Divine." But whatever the reason, his new-found love of opera survived the disappointments of the Boston trip, and in 1888 he organized Stephens's Opera Company, producing in quick succession *The Bohemian Girl, Martha,* and *The Daughter of the Regiment.* Stephens produced some of the first, if not *the* first, fully staged operas between Chicago and San Francisco, selecting works which could be appreciated even by unsophisticated audiences.

In 1889, the Church finally allowed the Tabernacle to be used for events with paid admissions. The Salt Lake Theatre could no longer provide the large performing space and audience capacity required by the touring groups which were already beginning to crisscross the country, and for which Salt Lake City was a logical stopping place. With the Tabernacle now available, the number and variety of musical events increased, making the nation's leading attractions available to local audiences. One of these led, indirectly, to Stephens's selection as conductor of the Tabernacle Choir.

One of the most enterprising of the nineteenth century's musicians was Patrick Sarsfield Gilmore—"The Great Gilmore," as he was quite properly known. During the Civil War he had been the bandmaster of the Union Army and had composed (or arranged) "When Johnny Comes Marching Home." After the war, Gilmore took up concert managing, with himself as the star, becoming famous for his giant musical extravaganzas. For the National Peace Jubilee of 1869 in Boston, Gilmore had engaged an orchestra of 1,000 and a chorus of 10,000, and had built a coliseum seating 50,000 to house the performance. When he toured with his band, showmanship was as much a part of his performance as was the music.

Learning that the Tabernacle was available for commercial engagements, Gilmore sent out an advance agent to book the hall and set up a "Gilmore Festival." A part of this festival was to be a large chorus prepared by a local musician. Asking around as to who could best create and direct a big chorus, the advance man was quickly and universally told: Evan Stephens.

Since Beesley's Tabernacle Choir of 150 was obviously too small, Stephens organized the Salt Lake City Choral Society, 400 members strong, which included many Tabernacle Choir singers but took its members from all faiths and occupations. Its two requirements: no discussion of politics and no talking about religion!

Gilmore's Grand Musical Festival was presented in the Tabernacle three times, featuring Stephens's choir in several selections, including the show's grand finale, "The Anvil Chorus" from Verdi's *Il Trovatore,* "combining chorus, Gilmore's band, artillery, etc."

The singers begged Stephens to continue the society as a permanent organization, and he immediately began to plan his own festivals: the First Annual Spring Festival in May 1890 was followed by a "June Festival" in 1891. His

A group photo of the Mormon Tabernacle Choir, with Evan Stephens, conductor, and Joseph Daynes, organist.

programs combined opera, oratorio, and instrumental selections and featured several of America's leading singers as guest artists.

In all the excitement, no one was paying any attention to the Salt Lake Tabernacle Choir. This was clearly an unacceptable state of affairs. To reestablish the Choir as the leading musical organization of Salt Lake City, the Church leaders turned to the man who had created—and could best solve—their dilemma. Evan Stephens assumed leadership of the Tabernacle Choir in 1890.

The new director already had a long association with the Choir, his countertenor voice having been heard in the alto section for years. Within six months, Evan Stephens increased the Choir's membership from 125 to more than 600, and the Choir area had to be redesigned to accommodate them. Stephens and Church architect Don Carlos Young (son of Brigham) collaborated on the new arrangement, which placed the choir seats in their present amphitheatric shape and roughly doubled the seating capacity. It also had the effect of markedly improving the acoustics of the building.

But not even Stephens's enthusiasm could rid him of the bane of every voluntary musical organization: recruitment was no problem, but regular rehearsal attendance was. Beesley's Choir had voted in 1881 to remove singers from the roll after being absent from four practices without sufficient excuse. Yet by the time Stephens succeeded Beesley, fewer than 300 members out of 600 would actually attend a rehearsal or performance. Singing in the Choir had not yet been recognized as an important Church service, having priority over conflicting duties. It was only after the Choir's dazzling success on tour in 1893 that such recognition became official Church policy.

A letter signed by President Wilford Woodruff and his Counselors, George Q. Cannon and Joseph F. Smith, written in 1895, said in part:

> Being called especially to this work, all other duties of a public nature should be secondary. None should be under obligation to perform any other public duty which would conflict with their duties in this Choir, unless first released from this Choir. . . . All those called to this work should be faithful in their attendance, and should give hearty and cheerful aid to the conductors; complying as far as possible with the plans and movements deemed necessary to the Choir's proper advancements toward perfection in the "divine art" which cannot be attained without united effort and perfect discipline. . . . This is a noble work, a glorious cause, worthy of your earnest efforts, and of the exertion it requires; as well as the exercise of the divine gifts and talents with which you are endowed. . . .

Unfortunately, even this official show of support did little to noticeably improve attendance. And so, on January 4, 1898, conductor Evan Stephens printed a public "New Year's Greeting" to the Choir in the *Deseret Evening News:*

> Fellow workers in the Divine Art—The new year is here to remind us of the renewal of all things. Many of you, through the press of other business and various causes have, for some time past, been lying dormant, and it becomes my duty, as the present gardener in charge, to send you greeting. The time has come

when you must awake and again send up sap. Let the buds of attendance break forth to show that there is still life within, and the promise of future bloom and fruit is sufficient to cause the trimming knife to pass you by. The garden must be put in order for the year 1898, and if by Sunday, January 16, no signs of life appear in you, (though there may have been in the past), it will be the secretary's duty to treat you as dead branches, erase your names from among the living branches, and place them among the "have beens."

. . . If you have been negligent in the late past, try to do better. There is no immediate prospect of an excursion to California, New York, or Paris. Now is your opportunity to renew diligence without seeming to have inartistic motives. . . .

The last decade of the nineteenth century was a propitious time for the Tabernacle Choir under its new and talented director. Stephens took up the baton in the year of the Manifesto against polygamy, and the Mormon society was no longer spending most of its energies defending itself from the federal government and other enemies. The Church's properties were released from federal control, and the campaign for statehood was rekindled, directing the Church's attention outward to the rest of the nation and the world. The great forty-year work of building the Temple was nearly finished.

Stephens's regime coincided with the availability of printed music in the Territory, greatly expanding the Choir's repertoire. And regular weekly rehearsals were now necessary to prepare for the Sunday afternoon meetings in the Tabernacle. These were not the conventional worship services which include sacraments, or Communion, but featured inspirational addresses by prominent visitors and civic leaders as well as Church leaders.

At these services, the Choir and organ performed hymns and anthems, and, although Stephens was not generally known for his tranquil relationships with colleagues, conductor and organist enjoyed almost perfect rapport. Joseph J. Daynes was proud that his organ student had become his conductor. Another of Daynes's pupils, Edna Corey Dyer, once said in a speech:

The perfect teamwork between Professor Stephens and his organist, Professor Joseph J. Daynes, was an example to every other chorister and organist in the church. I've heard each one say that their ideas of the interpretation of music seemed identical, and of course, there was always mutual admiration and respect.

The Choir was also included in many of the concerts which the traveling luminaries of the music world scheduled in the Tabernacle, with consequent enrichment of the members' musical experience. Many visiting artists also engaged the Tabernacle organist to serve as their accompanist. The result was almost a surfeit of musical riches—too many concerts to attend. When the Choir was on one program at the Tabernacle, singers had to be reminded to let a competing event in the Salt Lake Theatre pass.

Among the noted artists to perform were Mademoiselle Charlotte Maconda,

Evan Stephens

the Conreid Opera Company, John Philip Sousa's band, the great vocalist Nordica, accompanied by the Metropolitan Opera Orchestra, Paderewski, and Dame Nellie Melba. Melba was a bit condescending about singing for the backward people of Salt Lake City. When she first was introduced to bachelor Evan Stephens, she inquired of him, "And how many wives do *you* have, Maestro Stephens?" He answered, "Not so many that I can't handle one more." Madame Melba's experience in Salt Lake City turned out to be an eye-opening one for her despite her initial misconceptions. When she arrived in the Tabernacle she was asked whether she might care to hear the Choir sing a piece for her. Stephens offered to conduct one of his best loved compositions, "Let the Mountains Shout for Joy." "I will listen to it because it is yours, Maestro Stephens," she replied, "not because it is Mormon." The Choir sang superbly. The final chord had not finished reverberating when Madame Melba ran up to the podium to embrace Stephens and thank him for the exquisite, moving experience he had just provided. When she left Salt Lake City after a most successful concert, she was quoted as saying that the *next* time she came to town she would stay at "bachelor Stephens's" house.

In 1893, the Choir participated in two special events which marked a culmination and another new beginning. The Salt Lake Temple was dedicated on April 6, 1893, and six months later the Choir made its first major concert tour.

Even more than in Kirtland and Nauvoo, the ceremonies surrounding the dedication of the Salt Lake Temple were filled with the joy of accomplishment and with a renewed spirit of hope and purpose. A year earlier, at the laying of the Temple's capstone, the Choir had sung pieces especially composed for the occasion, and then the sixty thousand people surrounding the Temple had shouted "Hosanna" and sung "The Spirit of God Like a Fire Is Burning," the hymn which had greeted the dedication of the Temple in Kirtland.

The dedication ceremonies took place inside the completed building, and all of the music used was by LDS composers. The Choir sang, "Let All Israel Join and Sing" by Joseph J. Daynes. The President and Prophet of the Church, Wilford Woodruff, delivered the dedicatory prayer. The Choir answered with the "Hosanna Anthem," especially composed for the dedication by Evan Stephens. (This anthem, which features music for the congregation as well as the Choir, has been used at every subsequent Temple dedication.) The congregants all waved handkerchiefs at the singing of the word *Hosanna*. The final anthem was "Arise Ye Saints," by Charles J. Thomas.

One of the members of the Choir that day was photographer C. R. Savage, a man whose energies and talents have given us many of our best views of life in early Utah. Savage wrote:

> Sang with the Choir in the first dedication ceremony in the Temple. Never in my life did I feel an influence like unto the one I felt during the ceremony—every heart was touched with the divinity of our surroundings. I never felt a better influence in my life. I never had more great joy than I felt—my soul was filled

with peace, and my whole nature replete with satisfaction. The ceremony lasted four hours. . . . I never felt nearer to the invisible powers than while in the Temple.

The ceremony was repeated many times during the next twelve days to accommodate the thousands of people who wanted to participate. Groups from the Tabernacle Choir sang at each of these ceremonies.

Two months after the dedication of the Temple, the Choir began preparing for an entirely new adventure.

The Choir boarding a train, at the Salt Lake City railroad station, to leave for
Chicago, 1893.

7

Emissaries

At ten after three on the afternoon of August 29, 1893, a pivotal event in the Mormons' relationships with the rest of the nation began. The 250 members of the Salt Lake Mormon Tabernacle Choir, plus 100 relatives and friends, boarded a special ten-car railroad train at the Union Pacific Station in Salt Lake City to travel halfway across America to Chicago.

The Choir had been on tour before this time. Their initial excursion away from Salt Lake City, to American Fork in 1880, was followed almost annually by similar trips to nearby counties. Beesley took the Choir to Provo in 1882, to Ogden in 1883, to Nephi in 1884, and to Tooele in 1885. But never before had they traveled out of the state.

Back across the miles from Utah to Illinois the Mormons rode, retracing the distance so many of them had walked decades earlier. This time, however, they were not refugees, but cultural ambassadors. The first pioneer wagons made the trip westward in 111 days; now, traveling eastward by rail, it took only six. Evan Stephens, the boy who had taken such delight in crossing the plains twenty-seven years earlier on foot, was now making his second railroad trip in the opposite direction. The Church President and his two counselors traveled with the Choir, occupying the railroad's most prestigious private car, the "Pickwick."

It was a trip that almost didn't happen.

Eighteen ninety-three had already been a busy year for the Choir. Following the dedication of the Salt Lake Temple, the Choir traveled on April 27 to Manti, Utah, for ceremonies marking the dedication of the new Temple there.

However, when three officials from Chicago formally invited the Choir to participate in the great Welsh singing contest (the Eisteddfod) at the Chicago World's Fair, the offer had to be turned down. Evan Stephens had already made plans to be away at that time, traveling in Europe. And even if Stephens did change his plans, the Choir lacked the money to make the trip to Chicago. The panic of 1893 had left the country in a depression, and there wasn't even the hope of raising the money—or so it seemed.

But the political and business leaders of the Salt Lake community recognized the greater purpose that such a trip could offer—winning friends for the Church, encouraging travel to Utah, and pressing the cause of statehood. By the next day, eight businessmen had formed a committee to take care of all the arrangements for a tour. As the *Deseret News* reported: "The unanimous opinion was that Utah could not afford to allow this opportunity to pass to show to the outside world something of her musical status and progress; further—that it would do more to advertise the Territory and to reflect more of the real conditions existing here than any sort of missionary work that could be attempted."

The business community of Salt Lake, Mormon and non-Mormon alike, pledged their contributions. Horace G. Whitney was selected to manage the tour. The committee would pay the railroad, furnish Pullman sleeping cars, and pay all board and lodging in Chicago and other stops. They would schedule concerts en route and charge admission. The Choir singers could expect no direct income, however—they sang for free. Today this remains the pattern of all Choir trips.

Choir members were tremendously excited. Of 350 people on the rolls, only 250 could be taken on tour. A selection had to be made and the names of those chosen were published in the daily newspaper. Choir member George Kirkheim recorded in his diary the tension that surrounded the day of the posting. "As soon as dawn broke," George wrote, "I rushed out to buy the morning *News Herald.* Before I could get my change I saw my name was placed at the very head of the basses. I shall never forget what my feelings were as I exclaimed (partly to myself, partly aloud), 'Thank God for that.' I felt 'O what a joy!' "

Evan Stephens selected eight vocal soloists and a string quartet led by the Christiansen Brothers and Willard Weihe, the greatest violinist of the Territory. Joseph J. Daynes and his assistant, Anton Pederson, a non-Mormon, were to accompany the Choir on piano and organ. A guest of the First Presidency was Mr. Thomas Radcliff, also a nonmember, who had abandoned a flourishing European concert career because of asthma and settled in Salt Lake City. He had quickly become an honored organist and teacher in the local musical community.

Before their departure from Salt Lake City, the Choir proudly performed their challenging program, on the afternoon and evening of August 25, at Salt Lake City's great summer resort, Saltair, on the shore of the Great Salt Lake. The next Sunday the tour managers sponsored a fund-raising "sacred concert" in the Tabernacle. It was heavily advertised, and the Union Pacific Railroad offered special rates to people from surrounding communities. The commercialism surrounding the affair and the rather loose use of the term *sacred* for a paid-admission affair on the Sabbath disturbed Thomas Griggs. He noted in his diary, "I did not feel well over the matter—I think it is a grand mistake. Enquiries are made as to when we will have a *sacred* baseball game. . . ."

Before they left, Choir members were given a list of do's and don't's to show that they were not, as so many easterners still believed, a collection of rude farmers and cowboys:

Never eat with your elbows sprawled on the table. Between courses, one elbow, not both, may be leaned upon.

Never dunk in public. At home go ahead.

Never place a whole piece of bread on the palm of your hand and slap butter on it with a house-painting technique. Bread should be broken enough for one mouthful at a time, buttering each piece as you break it. Rolls and buns the same way.

FINGERS OR FORKS?

Bacon: If it's crisp, eat with fingers rather than scatter like confetti by trying to cut it. But use knife and fork if you like your bacon soft.

Cake: Dry cake may be broken and eaten in small pieces, but soft or sticky cakes need the fork.

French fried potatoes: Cut in half with the fork, if necessary—then eat with fork, not fingers. I know, I know; but it's the way it's done.

Armed with this impeccable advice, the Choir was ready to take on the "civilized" world.

The concert programs were built around the three selections for the full Choir and three more for the men's chorus which were prepared especially for the competition in Chicago, with vocal solos and duets and instrumental selections added. Stephens's composition for the women's chorus, "Mother's Lullaby," was the only American or Mormon music in the tour repertoire. Stephens and this Choir from the "wild West" chose European music rather than music by "home composers" of which the singers could have been justly proud. It was a highly respectable, thoroughly "classical" program: nothing backwoods about it. The tour program was very definitely for soloists. Of the numbers not required by the Chicago festival, five were for solo singers and one for the vocal quartet with chorus accompaniment. (When today's conductor, Jerold Ottley, recently programmed several soprano solos in a Choir program, he was renewing an earlier Choir custom.)

More than 3,000 people cheered and the Saltair Band serenaded as the train pulled out. "THE BIGGEST EXCURSION EVER TO LEAVE SALT LAKE CITY!" read the headlines. Emblazoned on a banner covering three consecutive cars and on badges worn by the singers was "MORMON TABERNACLE CHOIR." Their badges bore an illustration not of their Tabernacle, but of the Salt Lake Temple.

The word *Mormon* was a nickname, often derisively used, to identify The Church of Jesus Christ of Latter-day Saints, derived from their volume of modern scripture, the *Book of Mormon.* Its use for the tour was significant: the Choir was ready to meet the world on its own terms, to show by their music and their lives that they were worthy of their most sacred symbol, the Temple. It was more than a singing group that left the station that day; it was the hopes of the people.

Traveling across Utah that Tuesday afternoon, the Choir was met by cheering crowds, official speeches, and brass bands. The Choir reciprocated by singing from their train windows or on the station platforms. At one stop the men took too long to sing a few numbers, and, as the last piece ended, the train started to pull out. One singer made it back on board only by jumping headfirst through an open window. His performance was the hit of the afternoon.

The Choir sang its first tour concert the next evening in Denver, changing into concert clothing on the train ("not without some difficulty") and taking coaches to the Trinity Methodist Episcopal Church.

Their first concert was a success. Music lovers and curiosity seekers were out in force. The concert was sold out and people who could not gain admission remained outside hoping to catch some of the sound from within. The audience was not disappointed. Wave upon wave of applause broke over the Choir following their performance of the contest pieces accompanied by organist and a small orchestra. The encores and applause lasted forty-five minutes. This performance signaled a most propitious success and set the tone for the entire tour.

Thursday was a travel day relieved by a stop along the way to watch several black folk-musicians perform a hoedown. Small-town musicians were often on hand at the railroad stations to play and sing for the passing trains. It wasn't often, however, that the town players were answered by songs bursting forth from the throats of 250 people. Later that day at Junction City, Kansas, the Choir met another train carrying the great actor Henry Irving and his company. The male chorus sang for the troupe, and were answered by heartfelt applause as the other train disappeared into the setting sun.

The train arrived that evening in Kansas City, where Choir members spent a restful night in their compartments. At nine o'clock the next morning the citizens of Independence, Missouri, the mayor and the city council among them, greeted the Choir and escorted them to Independence, where Choir members were given a tremendous reception. Fifty years earlier, their parents had been driven out of their Missouri homes by mobs. Now fifty carriages met them to take the singers to the site where their parents had planned to build a temple. Many Choir members, however, chose to walk up the shaded hill to their destination. The citizens of Independence, wrote Griggs, "were respectful . . . and anxious to please and entertain." Banners waved and the Temple Hill was resplendent in summer glory.

The mayor invited the Salt Lake City visitors to the church which the members of The Reorganized Church of Jesus Christ of Latter-day Saints had built near the original Temple site. (The Reorganized Church was formed in 1860 among Mormons who did not move west with Brigham Young's pioneers.)

The Choir left Independence at noon, happy and spiritually charged. The next day the *Kansas City Times* published a lengthy article under the banner headline: "THIS TIME A FRIENDLY MOB!" The *Times* article was precisely the sort of response which the Choir's leaders hoped to achieve from their tour. The paper presented a calm, unbiased, factual discussion of the history of Mormonism and its beliefs.

Matinee and evening concerts in Kansas City and another triumphant performance in St. Louis the following evening helped to hone the Choir for the competition in Chicago. More than 3,500 attended in St. Louis, where the *Globe-Democrat* reported:

> The voices displayed before the audience of last evening are of the best. . . . Good as they evidently are by nature, they have received no little benefit from the careful culture received at the hands of Conductor Stephens. . . .
>
> There was what is often lacking in concerts of professional people, a spirit of enthusiasm among the singers that more properly rendered the chosen selection than could have been done by professional skill alone. But when to the skill of the professional is added the enthusiasm of the amateur the result is perfection. . . .
>
> There was a lack of conventionality in the concert that both surprised and pleased the hearers. The leader read the program in an old-fashioned style that both interested and amused the people; he pulled the conductor's stand from the platform with an energy that showed he was accustomed to wait on himself; he forgot to bow on entering and on leaving, and generally exhibited unfamiliarity with the tricks of a professional conductor. But so far from being offended the change was evidently agreeable to the audience and they applauded his old-time ways as heartily as they would have done the most Chesterfieldian bow that was ever made from a platform.

The audience, typical of the patrons who always come to Choir performances, was comprised of regular concertgoers and of the people who enjoy music of quality but are usually put off by the concertgoing ritual.

The next morning the singers awoke on the train to the first Sunday in many years that they would not be performing in the Tabernacle. Back home, the Choir members who were left behind were joined by singers from ward choirs in the valley. C. J. Thomas came out of retirement to conduct, and there were almost as many singers as usual in the Tabernacle.

A featured tour soloist was Nellie Druce Pugsley, a close friend of Evan Stephens, who was also her accompanist; both had been reared in the Utah culture. She had played the family melodeon which had been brought across the plains and started formal singing lessons at fifteen. She had given birth to one of her ten children six weeks before the choir tour, and both the baby and a baby-sitting sister went along, the infant receiving her christening blessing aboard the train. Of the mother's singing, a Chicago paper wrote:

> The leading soprano in the Choir is Nellie Druce Pugsley, a native of Salt Lake. The range of her voice seems almost unlimited, from high D to A-flat below the

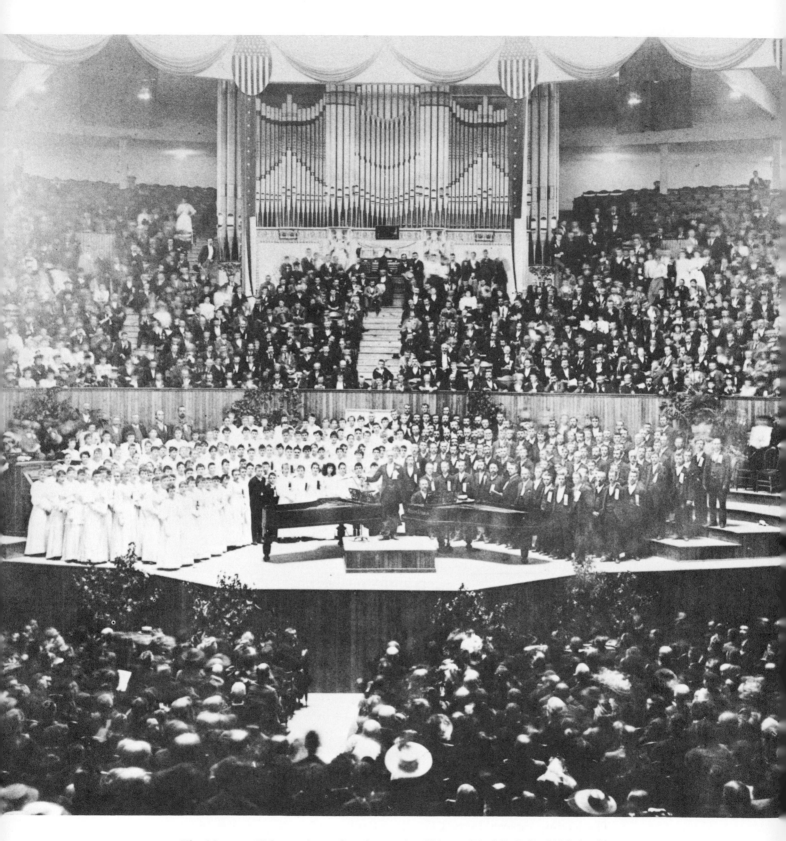

The Mormon Tabernacle performing at the Chicago World's Fair, 1893, in the
Eisteddfod competition.

staff being the easy scope for her exceptionally pure voice, which many musicians pronounce the exact counterpart of Lillian Norton, better known as Nordica, the famous Boston favorite.

The Choir arrived in Chicago Sunday afternoon and, before the contest the following Friday, rehearsed daily. Much to their surprise, Choir members found themselves one of the leading tourist attractions at the fair. The badges they wore excited such attention that many singers were arriving late for rehearsals; Stephens banned them from being worn.

The Chicago World's Fair was a paean to the creative inventiveness of humanity and a showcase for America's cultural achievement. "The fair," wrote C. R. Savage, "eclipses all my previous opportunities of seeing the skill of man." The directors of the fair sponsored a choral competition called the Eisteddfod, a traditional Welsh "gathering of the bards." The Welsh were as closely associated with choral singing in 1893 as they are today. But this Eisteddfod was arranged so that the public could also have a taste of the high level of *American* choral singing. Four mixed choirs were participating in the contest—the Western Reserve (Ohio) Choral Union, the Cymrodorion Society from Scranton, Pennsylvania, the Scranton Pennsylvania Choral Union, and the Mormon Tabernacle Choir.

The male chorus competition took place on Tuesday. Competing choirs included two from Wales, which took the first and second prizes. The Mormon men "were rated third, thus making us first, this side of the ocean," according to Griggs's diary.

The day of the contest arrived. There were prayers and whispered encouragements, and Evan Stephens gave his final instructions to the Choir: "Pay no attention to your competitors until you have sung, be not eager to excel them. Simply be calm, earnest, and see to it that we do ourselves justice, and I for one, will be satisfied, prize or no prize."

The Choir ascended to the stage, "250 strong, being warily greeted by the large and intensely interested audience," as Griggs later wrote. They assumed their positions and posed for photographs.

The three contest pieces took about twelve minutes to perform. "Considerable applause," came from the audience of 7,000 people when it was over. Most of the Choir members stayed to listen to the other choruses perform, and were disturbed to find that the two choirs from Scranton had recruited some of the Welsh singers to swell their ranks.

At the end of the contest, the Tabernacle Choir joined the others for a final gala performance of the "Hallelujah Chorus," which Evan Stephens was invited to conduct.

The chief judge, Dr. John Henry Gower, looked about the hall and finally announced that, "Taking all things together the two choirs which sang with the fewest faults and the most excellencies were, first, the Choral Union, from Scranton, and the Tabernacle Choir, from Salt Lake City."

Pandemonium broke loose. The Pennsylvanians yelled and the Salt Lake City people cheered. Finally one of the Scranton folks called out, "Three cheers for the Mormons!" and the shouts resounded even louder.

Wrote Second Counselor (later, President) Joseph F. Smith from Chicago to his wife, Sarah Ellen Richards Smith, back home in Salt Lake City:

> You will have heard before this reaches you that the Choir got the 2nd prize in the great contest at the World's Fair. The fact is they won the 1st prize, but as I feared all the while public sentiment would not permit them to carry it away. There is not a shadow of a doubt in the minds of many that the Choir won the prize fairly and honestly, but two of the three judges would not consent for them to get the 1st prize which would have put them at once at the top of the ladder of choral singing—This was too much honor to confer upon Utah and the Mormons! So they only awarded them the 2nd prize—$1,000—but could not say one word against them, except that they did not throw enough "Soul" into their music. But that they threw the most harmony and sweetness into it, they all acknowledged. One of the judges was pronounced and emphatic in favor of the Tabernacle Choir, but the other two were too much for him. It is a glorious triumph anyway to Utah and the "Mormon" people. And the good seed sown will be a good fruit in a day to come.
>
> Many a one has had his eyes opened, somewhat, on Utah, and the Mormon question. I consider it has done more good than five thousand Sermons would have done in an ordinary or even in an extraordinary way.

"It has done more good than five thousand Sermons would have done." In these words is the key to one of the major reasons for the continued emphasis, support, and encouragement which the Church has given to the Choir from 1893 to the present.

President Smith was probably reading more anti-Mormon prejudice into the final results of the contest than was really there. The Choir's performance was by no means perfect; in particular they "flatted" in several spots, especially at the ends of pieces. The next evening the Choir sang in downtown Chicago and this was generally judged to be a better performance. One of the contest officials said, "Had the Mormon Choir sung as well at the great contest as they did on the Saturday after at the Grand Central Music Hall, they would have easily defeated all competitors."

The members of the Choir were more than content with their victory. They had the satisfaction that they were judged the best choir with totally American personnel and they got to bring home a prize of $1,000. It had taken the Welsh to defeat them. The Tabernacle Choir's contest performance was such a success that they were offered an East Coast tour beginning immediately with stops in Boston, Philadelphia, Washington, and Carnegie Hall in New York. The Choir reluctantly declined; they had commitments to honor in Chicago and on the way back to Utah.

The Choir boarded the train immediately after their Saturday concert and headed for Omaha, arriving two hours after the scheduled start of the concert. The Choir went to "the opera house weary and hungry, and sang indifferently, to the audience who had been awaiting our arrival for over two hours." Griggs's comment underscores a dilemma that has confronted subsequent tours as well; scheduling has sometimes been too tight. The high costs of touring and the desire to perform for as many people as possible in the shortest period of time can be unfair to audiences and to the Choir.

The Omaha concert was the final tour performance, after which the Choir continued the journey back to Utah. Late at night, they passed through Castle Gate, Colorado, where a lone stationmaster was the only person to be seen. Nevertheless, he was serenaded by the whole Tabernacle Choir—he and the rugged mountain range which was the Choir's home. When they stopped to enjoy the thermal baths at Glenwood Springs, Colorado, news came to a member of the Choir that one of her children was very ill. The other members sacrificed the remaining hours of their well-deserved rest to rush home for the sake of Sister Bessie Dean Allison. When the train pulled into Salt Lake City, it was too early for brass bands, too early for crowds, just time for the sleepy, tired, happy Choir members to stumble to their houses and greet their families.

The Choir's victory fired the popular imagination, and was seen as an historic justification for years of suffering. Stephens received praise with his usual forthrightness: "I have learned but one thing of my Choir, they can do themselves justice under fire, and I am proud of them." Their late decision to enter had given them only three months to prepare music other choirs had been studying for more than a year.

Five more tours followed during Stephens's regime. Although he described a northern California tour in 1896 as a "pleasure trip," the Choir performed in Oakland on April 14, 1896, followed by concerts in San Francisco's Metropolitan Hall on the fifteenth, sixteenth, seventeenth, and eighteenth, a performance of all sacred music on the nineteenth and concerts in San Jose on the twentieth and Sacramento on the twenty-first. That same year, the Choir traveled to the Eisteddfod held in Denver; this time they won.

Another northern California "pleasure trip" was booked in 1902. In 1909, the Alaska-Yukon Pacific Exposition Eisteddfod attracted the Choir enough to plan a tour to Seattle, visiting Idaho, Washington, and Oregon concert halls on the way. But after they arrived, they refused to participate in the competition when they learned it would cost every Choir member seventy-five cents just to file in, sing their number, and leave. However, they still sang a full concert in the exposition's amphitheater to enthusiastic applause and rave reviews.

8

Welcome Century

FOR FIFTY-THREE YEARS the Tabernacle Choir had sung primarily to encourage, sustain, and inspire the membership of the Church as they struggled to establish their new Zion. In the century that was just beginning, the Choir would perform more and more for audiences of non-Mormons, both at home and on tour, and eventually for millions they would never meet.

The missing ingredient in all the Choir's trips was, of course, its own magnificent Tabernacle organ. However, the railroads were now making it possible for an ever increasing number of visitors to come to Salt Lake City. The majestic Temple and the Tabernacle with its organ and Choir made Temple Square the city's major public attraction.

A brilliant young homegrown organist, John J. McClellan, succeeded Joseph J. Daynes at the turn of the century, and regular public organ recitals soon followed. Twice in the next fifteen years the organ would be rebuilt, and Stephens and McClellan would use an important new medium of performance to reach an unseen audience: recordings.

John J. McClellan, the man who first made the Salt Lake Tabernacle organ nationally famous, was also the first important Mormon musician born and raised in Utah. In his birthplace of Payson, his first musical experience was singing in the ward choir. Shortly after, he began organ lessons and was soon his ward's organist and the local dance band's pianist.

By the time he was sixteen he had exhausted the possibilities of local music teachers and enrolled in the newly created Conservatory of Music at the University of Michigan. A strong organizational ability quickly manifested itself in McClellan, and in one year he founded and was conducting the University of Michigan Symphony Orchestra. He also directed and managed a dance orchestra and worked as a paid choir director and organist at several (non-LDS) churches.

McClellan was graduated in 1896, and returned to Utah, where he spent half of each week as the director of music at the Latter-day Saints College in Salt Lake City and half as the director of music of the Brigham Young Academy (now University) in Provo, forty-five miles away.

Three years later, McClellan was traveling again, this time with his new family and Berlin as his destination. There he was trained in the solid German tradition by Xaver Scharwenka and Ernest Jelienzka, two of the era's great teachers. His year in Berlin was soon put to good use. He returned to Utah just before the resignation of Joseph Daynes and in 1900, at the age of twenty-six, was appointed organist of the Salt Lake Tabernacle, a position he would hold for the rest of his life.

McClellan was as active in Salt Lake as he had been during his student days at the University of Michigan.

Teaching took up a great amount of his time, both privately and at the Church-sponsored McCune School of Music. He founded and conducted the Mendelssohn Club, a male chorus, and was the director of the first performance of Mendelssohn's *Elijah* in the Salt Lake Valley, under the auspices of the Salt Lake City Choral Society. McClellan also became a theater organist, directed dance bands at the fashionable Hotel Utah, and was organist for the Salt Lake City Christian Science Church.

With all these activities, he still found time to play the organ at the Tabernacle. Like Daynes before him, McClellan was "on call" to give recitals for visiting dignitaries, often at very short notice. Sometimes the people so honored were quite out of the ordinary. Edna Corey Dyer, a pupil of Daynes and McClellan who also performed at Tabernacle recitals, wrote of one such occasion: "There was a large organ recital given by J. J. McClellan (assisted by Mr. H. S. Goddard and Miss Lucy Gates, singers) in honor of Buffalo Bill's Wild West Show." Eight thousand people were present for the recital, "perhaps not so much for the love of music as curiosity to see Col. W. F. Cody with his long gray hair and stately dignity."

Daynes had struggled with the impromptu nature of the organ recitals, fighting for a regular schedule to which visiting dignitaries could bend their itineraries. McClellan also proposed that regular (at first biweekly, later daily) recitals for the general public be established. Even though it would require a good deal of money to heat and light the Tabernacle every Tuesday and Thursday, and although no proceeds were to be received from the recitals, the suggestion was approved by the General Conference on April 8, 1906. When concerts became a daily affair, the dilemma of applause on Sunday reared its head. On a Sunday recital in 1903, an applauding audience had to be stopped by officials. In 1913, McClellan concluded a fine recital one hot, summer Sunday, and a tourist stood up to speak. He said he regretted that applause was not allowed, and explained that in his native Texas, "in public gatherings where we are not allowed to applaud, we have a habit of waving our handkerchiefs. I now take the liberty to ask the audience to pay the organist this well-deserved tribute, as a token of our deep appreciation of this wonderful playing." And they did.

McClellan's public recitals were performed both for tourists who were not always acquainted with classical music and those who were extremely knowledgeable, and the organist had to hold the interest of both groups. McClellan accepted this challenge and rose to it, scheduling "classical pieces" and more popular tunes on the same program. Alexander Schreiner, a pupil of McClellan, once wrote: "[McClellan] said, 'I play to the ploughman,' and he did this both eloquently and poetically."

The bulk of the organist's repertoire was made up of transcriptions from the standard Romantic orchestral works, operas, and songs. There were a handful of popular pieces by Bach, and then, chronologically, nothing until Mendelssohn. A thoroughly Romantic organist, in the true nineteenth-century grand manner, McClellan firmly believed in the performer's right and duty to inject his own personality and temperament into the composition he was playing. And like the great Romantic players, he approached the organ as if it were an orchestra.

Since its installation, the organ had developed several mechanical problems, mostly through a third of a century of hard use, poor maintenance, and the limitations of the original design by Joseph Ridges. When McClellan was appointed Tabernacle organist, he immediately "perceived the sore necessity of effecting some radical changes and improvements in the organ, in order to make it a modern instrument, and to relieve the players from the handicap under which they had labored." On February 19, 1901, the aged Ridges was given a testimonial benefit, at which the old organ he had conceived and brought into being was heard for the last time; for the Tabernacle organ was about to be completely rebuilt.

The new organ was installed by the Kimball Company and was equipped with a tubular pneumatic action. Two-thirds of the pipes of the old organ were replaced, and the console was moved, taken out some fifty feet from its position under the pipes and turned around so that it faced the conductor. Because Kimball officials felt that McClellan was not acquainted enough with the new organ to show it off to its full advantage, and because this installation was so important to the company, they brought their own organist, Dr. George W. Walter, from a Washington, D.C., synagogue, to give the first recital on the instrument. The new organ was not without its critics, among them Evan Stephens, who said it lacked the sweetness of tone of the Ridges-Johnson organ.

In any case, the Kimball organ was to last only fifteen years, a victim of advancing technology and changing taste. Nor was the organ particularly well cared for. One Sunday in 1903, Edna Corey Dyer arrived at the Tabernacle ready to accompany the Choir to find that "in warming the building the fireman had turned steam into the open pipes and filled the console full of steam. Everything was dripping wet—wood mechanisms swollen and metalwork rusted so that keys were sticking down on all the manuals." What was worse, the accident happened again the next Sunday, so that during one of the hymns the second highest note and one of the pedals stuck throughout an entire piece. It is no surprise that by 1915 the *Deseret News* could complain about parts of the organ being worn out after only fifteen years of service.

In 1914 McClellan and Tracy Y. Cannon, the assistant organist, sent a letter to the First Presidency of the Church, in which they discussed the deteriorating condition of the organ and recommended that it be reconstructed by the Austin Organ Company of Hartford, Connecticut. By 1915, after suitable investigation, the First Presidency decided to proceed with the rebuilding.

The new Austin organ was the first instrument to use an electrical system which connects the keyboard to the pipes. In addition, the company greatly expanded the existing instrument. The Ridges and Kimball organs had consisted only of the center section of the present organ. The rebuilding preserved the original casework and added two side wings, each fifteen feet wide, which harmonized with the earlier design. The new pipes and divisions were voiced according to the organ-building philosophy of the times, having an elaborate string section and stressing sweetness of tone. By this time only about eight ranks of pipes from the original set were still in use.

McClellan helped put the Tabernacle on the map of great musical centers, not only through his own superb playing, but through the performance of his pupils. One of these was Edna Corey Dyer, an independent woman who was inspired by a visiting organist, Mrs. Annie Peat-Fink of Milwaukee—a musician of true ability. "I was delighted to know that a *woman* could really learn to play the *pipe-organ* well, hence I could take up my own labors with renewed energy." She resolved that evening to practice daily, even if she had to "disturb a few score of tourists by my (to them) meaningless racket." McClellan also taught a young German immigrant named Alexander Schreiner, who became one of the great organists of the twentieth century.

In 1905, a third student, Edward P. Kimball, had been appointed Tabernacle organist to assist McClellan. He had studied with his teacher as a young man, and had then gone to Germany, where he worked with Leopold Godowsky. Kimball represented a new style of playing and programming. He was the first organist in the Tabernacle to eschew opera and popular arrangements, concentrating instead on music which had actually been composed for the instrument. "He was only for the classics," his son remembers. Kimball performed on the first radio broadcast of the Choir, both as soloist and accompanist. Like all organists at the Tabernacle, he was responsible to the Choir, performing for both rehearsals and concerts, and it would be his good fortune to play for the Choir's first nationwide radio broadcast in 1929. In 1933, his career at the Tabernacle ended with his appointment as director and organist at the Washington, D.C., LDS Chapel.

In their work as musical emissaries of the Church, Evan Stephens and John J. McClellan were the first to use acoustical recordings to share the sounds of the Tabernacle Choir and organ with the millions of people who couldn't come to Salt Lake to see them.

The Choir sang for the Columbia Phonograph Company, which was a forerunner of Columbia Records. The "acoustical process," although substantially improved, was basically the same method of recording invented by Thomas A. Edison in 1877. Musical sound waves were collected by a large horn and focused on a taut, flexible diaphragm. Attached to it was a needle, placed on a warm, wax disc which rotated on a turntable and into which the needle made fluctuating indentations.

Recordings of the Tabernacle Choir and organ have always taxed the skills of technicians, because of the massive sounds and the spatial relationships involved. With acoustical records, the sounds closest to the horn came through loudest, as did the middle ranges of sounds; altos and, particularly, tenors sounded better than sopranos and basses. McClellan played the organ as loudly as possible, but was barely audible. Soloists put their heads right inside the horn.

Thirteen selections were recorded on September 1, 1910, featuring four organ pieces, two Choir numbers with vocal soloists, and seven by the Choir; Stephens chose four original works by "home composers" (two were his own) along with three choral standards by Handel and Gounod. Joseph J. Daynes came out of retirement to record one of the organ solos. Four additional organ recordings by McClellan were made the following day. The vocal artists were Mrs. Lizzie Thomas Edward, a soprano soloist on the Chicago tour of 1893, and baritone Horace Ensign, who was also assistant conductor of the Choir.

The recordings give scant idea of how the Choir and organ must have actually sounded, although it is apparent that the singers were considerably less cultivated than today's Choir. The Choir sounds like a large, well-trained revival chorus. Stephens used colossal retards at the ends of each phrase of a hymn, strong tempo contrasts, and a very wide dynamic range. His conducting is heartfelt, warm, outgoing, tremendously dramatic though sometimes a bit obvious and overly bombastic; however, the excitement of his work is tremendous.

The solo organ recordings are not representative of the old Kimball organ. The discs reproduce only the eight-foot stops; the higher and lower registers come through weakly, or not at all. The acoustical process could not reproduce room resonance, so that the organ sounds like an overgrown calliope. McClellan's musicianship comes across very clearly, however, and one perceives a major Romantic musical intelligence at work. His sense of rubato is quite elegant and his technical prowess distinguished. It is to be regretted that McClellan did not live long enough to have the benefit of more adequate sound for his recording ventures.

The capstone of Stephens's career was his last, and grandest, concert tour, to the major cities along the East Coast in 1911. The Choir was invited to perform for the American Land and Irrigation Exposition in New York City. (Utah was famous for its pioneer irrigation and water conservation projects.) George D. Pyper, the Choir's business manager for the trip, lined up other engagements at places famous in Latter-day Saints' history: Omaha, near Winter Quarters, Nebraska (by 1911 called Florence); Toledo, near Kirtland, Ohio; Rochester, near Palmyra, New York. The Choir's trip took the members back into their own history.

Once at the Exposition in New York, the Choir sang the *Ode to Irrigation,* a thirty-minute piece composed by John J. McClellan especially for this occasion, three times a day for ten days in the old Madison Square Garden. They also presented a different concert every evening in the garden's Concert Hall, exhausting "our entire repertoire of choruses," wrote Pyper. They capped their New York engagements by appearing twice at one of the city's grandest musical establishments, the Hippodrome.

After New York, the Choir presented a command concert in the White House in Washington, D.C., for President William Howard Taft, his wife, and about fifty guests. The concert for the president was a signal to the nation of the value which this country placed on religious freedom. The years 1910 and 1911 had witnessed a particularly virulent recurrence of anti-Mormon sentiment. Hall managers had refused to book the Choir in several cities; in other places, campaigns had been organized to discourage attendance at the concerts. The president's invitation was a clarion call that religious prejudice would not be tolerated in the United States.

For twenty-six years, from his appointment in 1880 until his retirement in 1916, Stephens's passion was the Tabernacle Choir. He had no family, few friends, and the Choir was the sole object of his devotion and his energies. The restlessness and vision of the man who guided the Choir from provincial to national prominence is reflected in his proposals for reorganizing the Choir. He wanted additional part-rehearsals twice a week. And he proposed choosing exemplary singers in each part to serve as models for their sections. He suggested an apprenticeship program for young singers ages ten to seventeen. He also campaigned for special well-lighted and -heated rehearsal facilities to be housed in the Tabernacle. He had an almost manic intensity concerning his beloved Choir and entertained unorthodox attempts at solving problems. A man of action and indomitable will, Stephens was able to grasp the difficulties he faced and give them a thorough shaking.

When asked to define what made music "Mormonistic," Stephens replied, "That which breathes optimism and not pessimism, music in which the somber must not predominate, but be used only as a means of contrast to heighten the effects of the bright." He composed special pieces for the fiftieth anniversary of the arrival of the first pioneers in Utah and a *Memorial Ode* for the one-hundredth birthday of Joseph Smith. He wrote an oratorio, *The Vision*, to commemorate the one-hundredth anniversary of Joseph Smith's first message from the Lord, and an audience of thousands came to hear the first performance of this piece. Stephens also composed "Utah, We Love Thee," which Utah officially chose as its state song on admission to the Union in 1896. Stephens always maintained that his own music reflected his pioneer origins and the pioneer life, for "it had a pinch of sagebrush in it." In 1916, the conductor's baton passed from Evan Stephens to the Choir's first Utah-born director, Anthony C. Lund.

At about this time, Edward P. Kimball was already alternating as Tabernacle organist with John McClellan—who sadly would die at the height of his career. Tracy Y. Cannon was assistant organist. Two other young organists, both of whom had already performed on Temple Square at early ages, were added to the

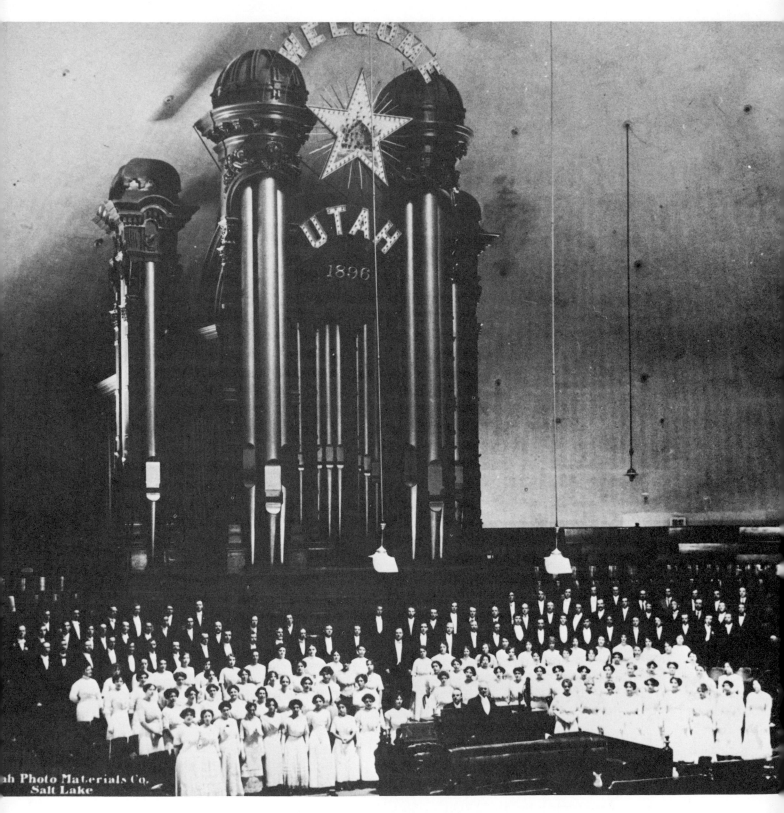

The Choir at the turn of the century, Evan Stephens conducting. The star and welcome banner to celebrate statehood were placed on the organ in 1896 and remained there for several years.

The Mormon Tabernacle at night

Temple Square in Salt Lake City

The illuminated Salt Lake Temple at left, with the Tabernacle in the background

Oakley S. Evans, president, and conductor Jerold D. Ottley with the Mormon Tabernacle Choir

The Tabernacle adorned with Christmas lights

Inside the Tabernacle

roster: the older of the two was Frank Asper; the younger, the immigrant *Wunderkind* Alexander Schreiner.

It was this new team of Mormon music makers who would carry on the Choir's concert tours, direct its next recordings, and, in 1929, launch the historic series of network radio broadcasts which would make the music of the Tabernacle Choir and organ accessible to virtually every home in the United States.

Tony Lund, born in the central Utah town of Ephraim, on February 25, 1871, was the director of the Mormon Tabernacle Choir from 1916 until his death in 1935. Several members of the Lund family were good amateur musicians, and Lund's aunt taught him to play the organ. He performed as singer and organist at the local church before being appointed the choir leader when he was eighteen. Upon graduation from Brigham Young University with a degree in music, he continued his education at the Leipzig Conservatory in Germany. In 1897, Brigham Young University appointed him to head its music faculty. In the following years, he returned briefly to France and England to study.

A consummate teacher, he helped train many of Utah's finest singers. He was a professor at the Utah Conservatory, and later at the McCune School of Music. The conservatory—owned and operated by the Church—was in what is still one of the most elegant buildings in Salt Lake City. It had been endowed by a wealthy railroad baron and became the center of musical pedagogy in the early twentieth century. Most of the period's major musicians passed through the school's substantial art deco doors as students or faculty, or both.

Anthony Lund was appointed the conductor of the Tabernacle Choir on July 28, 1916. By all reports, he was a superb musician. His few records reveal a conductor with straightforward, uneccentric ideas about tempos and phrasing. His Choir sounds much more in the European mold than Stephens's (based on the latter's 1910 recordings). The voices sound trained and the ensemble resembles one of the professional opera choruses of the day.

The Choir's 1927 recordings were made by the Victor Company of Camden, New Jersey. This time, the "electrical" recording process utilized microphones and amplifiers to convert acoustical energy into electrical impulses. The electrical recordings were an enormous improvement in terms of sound, fidelity, and ease of recording. On these recordings, for the first time, one can hear how the Choir and organ actually sounded. Lund was a most cultivated musician and his work can be heard tellingly here. In "He Watching over Israel," from Mendelssohn's *Elijah* and "Worthy Is the Lamb," from *Messiah,* Lund shaped the phrases in a fine, straightforward manner; the Choir's diction was very crisp (even though very American, with many hard *r*'s) and the basic tone was beautiful, the voices sounding much more cultivated than on the earlier recordings.

Judging only from these recordings, Lund's conducting did not possess the elemental excitement of Stephens's, but he excelled in music which requires control and subtlety. The best recording of the set is Samuel Coleridge-Taylor's "By the Waters of Minnetonka"; the delicate shadings and finely spun choral singing are most beautiful.

Alexander Schreiner

"I've been organist for the Church since the age of eight, and this is the greatest thing I can say about myself." Alexander Schreiner, Tabernacle organist from 1925 to 1977, is the man who has had the most influence in this century on making the music of the Tabernacle organ an internationally known phenomenon.

Schreiner was born in 1901 in Nuremberg, Germany. He was playing piano at the age of five; the organ followed soon after. Schreiner had memorized most of the music in the LDS hymnal by the time he was seven. He wanted to be the organist for his Latter-day Saints congregation in Germany, but, following the doctrines of the Church, young persons cannot be baptized until they are eight, "the age of accountability." Dr. Schreiner remembers, "They didn't want an unbaptized heathen as their organist." He had to wait a year to begin his service at the organ bench and a career which was to make him arguably the most renowned musician the Mormons have yet produced.

His family arrived in Salt Lake City on a Friday in 1912. By Sunday evening, he had a position as organist. He heard the organist during services Sunday morning. That afternoon she was not available, so young Schreiner volunteered his services. "Of course, I was better," he recalled, and he got the job.

As a young man in high school he could not decide whether to become an electrical engineer, a violinist, or an organist. John J. McClellan guided him toward the organ and Charles W. Nibley, at that time Presiding Bishop of the Church, fixed his course irrevocably toward music. Upon graduation from high school, he worked as a theater organist, which enabled him to save enough money to go on a mission for his Church to southern California. When he returned, he went to McClellan for organ lessons and two years later joined his mentor on the bench as a Tabernacle organist.

Continuing his studies in Europe, he went to France rather than to Germany, as McClellan had done. He studied with Louis Vierne at Nôtre Dame in Paris and also with Charles Marie Widor. Their music has figured prominently in his repertoire ever since.

Returning to his post at the Tabernacle in 1926, he began giving recitals and accompanying the Tabernacle Choir. Four years later, he was invited by the University of California at Los Angeles to join their music faculty and was appointed a professor of music, even though up to that time he had never spent a day in college. Dr. Ernest C. Moore, the university's provost, declared, "A genius like that needs no academic recommendation." He remained at the university for ten years, returning during the summers to Salt Lake City to give recitals and accompany the Choir. Schreiner was also organist for the Wilshire Boulevard Synagogue in Los Angeles and at Graumann's Metropolitan Theater.

Finally, in 1939, he returned to full-time work in Salt Lake City, and began to create his enviable reputation through his thousands of recitals and broadcasts. Schreiner still enjoyed a busy international career as a recitalist, playing throughout Europe and the United States, but no matter how attractive the life of an internationally famous musician may have seemed to him on occasion, he remained loyal to the Tabernacle and the Tabernacle Choir

Frank Asper

and always retained it as the center of his professional life.

The Tabernacle Choir loved working with him. His accompaniments were models of sensitive registration and strong rhythmic underpinning. Choir members recall with particular delight his impish "entertainments" during intervals in rehearsals, recording sessions, and, especially, between "takes" in television and motion picture productions, when the singers could not leave their seats.

On one occasion, sensing their growing discontent during the long wait, Schreiner cranked up an impromptu caricature with the organ the likes of which few had ever heard before, or since. Television jingles, popular songs, and dissonant harmonies were woven together, and he created marvelously comic effects by using outrageous combinations of stops. There was hearty laughter throughout the performance, and a rousing cheer greeted its conclusion. When the cameras were ready, so were the singers, refreshed by the surprise performance.

In 1954 Schreiner earned his doctorate, submitting a Concerto for Organ and Orchestra as his dissertation. It was the first doctorate of music granted by the University of Utah.

Schreiner has an impressive array of honorary degrees and citations (a Doctorate of Humane Letters from the University of Utah, a Doctorate of Fine Arts from Utah State, an Officers Cross of the Order of Merit for distinction in the performing arts, awarded by the West German government).

Frank W. Asper, appointed as a Tabernacle organist only three weeks after Schreiner, retired in 1965 after a distinquished career of forty-one years. He recorded several organ albums, played for more than a thousand network choir broadcasts—plus a weekly organ broadcast of his own—and performed approximately 5,000 organ recitals for visitors on Temple Square. In addition, he published several volumes of organ compositions, founded and conducted the 105-piece McCune Symphony Orchestra for three decades, and left his mark on thousands of students, including Tabernacle organist Roy M. Darley.

He learned to play on a melodeon that his father had brought across the plains in a covered wagon. At seven, he played the piano accompaniment to solos performed by his teacher, Ebenezer Beesley, and later played his first organ solo in the Assembly Hall on Temple Square when he was twelve. He studied three years in Berlin at Stern's Conservatory. Next, he went to Boston for five years, graduating with honors from the New England Conservatory, and was invited to remain as an instructor. He studied under Alberto Jonas, Giuseppe Buonamici, and George Whitefield Chadwick. He was awarded an honorary Doctor of Music degree from Bates College in 1938.

Although he was uncompromising in his own standards of performance, Dr. Asper was nevertheless a generous and patient teacher, who held free group classes for amateur organists and choristers to upgrade the musical standards for Mormon congregations and choirs throughout the Church. He founded and was dean of the Utah Chapter of the American Guild of Organists, of which he was a Fellow.

Both Schreiner and Asper wrote several hymns, and helped to produce the modern LDS hymnal. Both have also made significant contributions to Utah's music through their students who succeeded them.

9

Marvelous Things

FIVE YEARS AFTER the first American radio station began to operate, radio listeners in Salt Lake City could tune in on the Thursday evening Tabernacle Choir rehearsals. In another four years, the entire nation could hear them—every week.

Salt Lake City's KSL-Radio had only one microphone, and broadcasting stopped while a technician carried it from the studio to the Tabernacle, a city block away. Once there, the microphone was held, Statue of Liberty style, by an engineer perched atop a ladder in front of the Choir.

After KSL became an affiliate of the National Broadcasting Company, receiving its network programs, station manager Earl J. Glade had an idea: he convinced first the Choir and then the officers of NBC that the Choir should do a nationwide broadcast every week. The first was aired Monday, July 15, 1929, from 3:00 to 3:30 in the afternoon. The series continues today, although it has moved to another network, and to another day and hour.

When they first began broadcasting nationally, KSL's engineers were worried about the Tabernacle's reverberation, considering it too "live" for proper pickup. Across the street from Temple Square is the Hotel Utah, which in 1929 was installing new carpeting. The old rugs proved to be a perfect means of damping the reverberation.

"Everyone was very nervous; we all felt as if we were walking on eggshells," recalls Ted Kimball, who, at the age of nineteen, was the announcer for this first broadcast. Ted had been working at KSL for three years; his father, Edward P. Kimball, was the Tabernacle organist accompanying the Choir. The engineer suspended the single microphone from the ceiling, and Ted had to climb a stepladder to reach it; the mike was "live" throughout the broadcast and he had to stay there the entire time. The chief engineer was in a room below the choir seats; NBC headquarters in New York informed him by telegraph when to start the program. He gave a hand signal to a man standing at the top of the stairs leading from the Tabernacle basement to the main floor, who, in turn, signaled Ted Kimball up on his ladder.

The program was evenly divided between three works performed by the Choir and three by the organist. The first broadcast was received by more than thirty radio stations and was a qualified success. The musical qualities of the Choir and organ were praised, but the sound was another matter. After a few minutes, the signal to New York was afflicted by line-hum and many stations cut off because of the unpleasant noise. Engineers solved the technical difficulties by the next week and the show became a paradigm of good sound, as well as good music.

Lund, who was the conductor at the time, was a large, robust man who could easily lose his temper. Listeners of the early broadcasts could often hear his foot-stampings on the podium when the Choir wasn't performing to his satisfaction. He was also a man of tremendous affection; he considered each member of the Choir a close personal friend. One Sunday, a former Choir member came back to Salt Lake City to visit; she planned to surprise the Maestro by sitting with the sopranos. Conducting the first piece of the broadcast, Professor Lund looked up and saw his old friend. As soon as the number was over (an organ solo followed) he bounded up the stairs to speak with the young lady and didn't notice when the organ piece ended. Organist Kimball began a hasty bit of improvising. Finally, a couple of tenors climbed up to the sopranos and escorted the director back down to his post.

The broadcasts continued for three years on the NBC network, the time and day varying from week to week. The programs were important enough to the community for employers to allow the singers time off whenever the broadcasts were scheduled. It was an awkward situation, nonetheless, and not conducive to building a substantial regular audience.

KSL switched its affiliation to the Columbia radio network in 1932. A Columbia vice-president and member of the Church, G. Stanley McAllister, had been instrumental in attracting KSL to the network. NBC tried to hold on to the broadcasts, but Columbia in turn offered a regular Sunday morning time slot.

The program format remained the same for the first year. The Choir and organist performed several numbers, each of which an announcer identified before it was performed. Ted Kimball announced the first four broadcasts, then left Salt Lake City to go on a mission for the Church. Several other announcers followed. Finally, a young man named Richard L. Evans was assigned to the job.

J. Spencer Cornwall, whose career as Choir conductor was contemporary with Evans's, says what was universally felt: "Richard L. Evans was one of the greatest men, *as a man,* that I have ever been with. He had more personality, and more good advice and more wisdom than anybody else." Alexander Schreiner, the great Tabernacle organist, says simply: "He was the Choir's patron saint."

Richard Louis Evans, whose calm and fatherly voice spoke to millions for forty-one years, was born on March 23, 1906. He grew up in a large, poor family, quickly acquiring the habit of hard work and dedication which was to be his for the rest of his life. He studied at the University of Utah, paying his way with a scholarship awarded for his high-school debating activities. After his second year

Richard L. Evans

of college, he went to England on a mission for the Church. There he met James E. Talmage, a member of the Council of the Twelve and a distinguished writer, who recognized Richard's abilities and appointed him associate editor of the *Millenial Star,* the Church's British magazine. Talmage was a rigorous pedagogue, and the apprenticeship instilled in Evans an approach to the craft of writing based on careful thought and ceaseless revision.

His mission completed, Richard Evans returned to Salt Lake City to complete his education. Looking for a job he could work around his university schedule, he learned that radio station KSL needed an announcer. Evans loved radio, its challenge and excitement, and he thrived in its environment. He had been working only seven months at KSL when he was assigned to the Tabernacle Choir broadcast. He was twenty-four. He continued to announce the broadcasts, producing and writing them as well, and in 1934 he received a national award as the best radio announcer of the previous year.

When he was thirty-two, Evans was invited by President Heber J. Grant to become a member of the First Council of the Seventy, one of the Church's highest governing bodies (the average age of the other members of the Council was sixty-five). He served in this capacity for fifteen years until called to be a member of the Council of the Twelve in 1953.

In the secular world, he was a member of the board of regents of the University of Utah, sat on the board of trustees of Brigham Young University, and was a member of the Utah State Board of Higher Education. An active Rotarian, he served as that organization's international president from 1966 to 1967.

Throughout a career of service to the public and to the Church, which he pursued with seemingly limitless energy and dedication, Evans never willingly missed a Sunday morning broadcast of the Tabernacle Choir. His devoted wife, Alice, once suggested to him that, with the press of other responsibilities and advancing age, it might one day be necessary for him to give up the broadcasts. "How would you feel if someone asked you to give up one of your children?" he asked.

Richard L. Evans created the "Music and the Spoken Word" broadcasts. The unique blend of spoken word and music, of quiet meditative passion, which has continued to be the hallmark of the program, is his monument. He had started, as had his predecessors, by simply announcing the titles of the compositions and identifying the station. As time went on, he began relating the title of the work or its text to some point of philosophy or morals. These were rarely labored and seemed a natural flow of ideas, springing from the music, finally evolving into a two-to-three-minute nondenominational sermon. Evans's talks were unique because of their incredible concentration; they were haikus of Christian thought. Yet they touched people so deeply that they often felt that he had spoken directly to them.

Evans insisted on broadcasting live, even if it meant that he would have to be picked up from a location thousands of miles distant from the Tabernacle. He wrote, produced, and broadcast the "Spoken Word" every week for forty-one consecutive years, without vacations, without ghostwriters. Not until the coming of television did many of his listeners learn one of the secrets which explained the intimacy of his voice: he continued to use an early, long-obsolete microphone, speaking into it from only an inch or two away.

Here is a typical "Spoken Word" message:

"Life is like playing a violin solo in public," said Baron Lytton, "and learning the instrument as one goes on." We are often inclined to judge people by the flaws in their performance. We are likely to judge a young person, for instance, by some foolish or inexperienced act or utterance. People have sometimes carried through life the stigma of a single remark they have made, while hundreds of constructive, intelligent remarks are not remembered.

This does not mean that what a person says or does is not significant, or that he should not be accountable for his speech and actions. But there is no perfection in any of us, and in many ways people differ principally in the percentage, so to speak, of their goodness or faults.

To use another figure, the percentage of so-called perfect diamonds is very, very small, yet there are many beautiful stones that have some slight flaws. But we don't discard the diamond for the flaw. At this point, however, the figure fails us, for people are not static. They change. They learn—often they repent, often improve—and if a person's performance is unacceptable at some point, this is not to say that it may not later improve. While we cannot set aside the laws of cause and effect or suspend the penalties of a poor performance, we must remember that people change and move—they can repent, and they can improve.

The violinist whose music performance we pay to hear performs for us only after going through a long, arduous preparation, with many imperfect notes and unpleasant sounds and with much faulty fingering. But this is usually without an audience, while much of our practice in learning how to live is out in the open. Life is for learning, for practicing and improving, and it is not always easy, as everyone knows. We all need understanding—especially the young—for so often we do our practicing in public.

The opening and closing announcements of "Music and the Spoken Word" are his trademark, like the sign-off lines of a famous newscaster or entertainer. Through many drafts and rewritings over the years, Evans finally settled on the form so familiar to the Choir's radio listeners even today: "Once more, we welcome you within these walls with music and the spoken word from the Crossroads of the West." The program's sign-off, too, was a distillation of years of experimentation and careful thought: "Again we leave you within the shadows of the everlasting hills. May peace be with you, this day and always."

Two generations of Mormon Tabernacle Choir members admired Richard L. Evans, but they also thought of him as their personal friend. Evans always accompanied them on tour, serving as announcer and commentator for their concerts. Instead of an intermission, the Choir would schedule five to ten minutes of Richard L. Evans. He was as good in front of a live audience as he was in front of a microphone. His unexpected death in 1972 was a loss keenly felt by Mormons and non-Mormons alike, all over the world. But few felt a stronger loss than the members of his beloved Tabernacle Choir.

The culmination of Anthony Lund's term as conductor came in 1934, only five years after the Tabernacle Choir network broadcasts began, bringing the Choir instant familiarity to millions throughout the land. The Choir was in its last year under his baton when Henry Ford, president of the Ford Motor Company, sponsored the Choir's participation in a series of twice-daily concerts in September 1934, in the Ford Symphony Gardens at the Century of Progress Exposition in Chicago. Concerts were scheduled in Independence and Denver during the return trip. A year later, for the California Pacific International Exposition in San Diego, the company again sponsored a series of concerts in the Ford Bowl at Balboa Park during the week of July 19. Under the baton of Acting Director Albert J. Southwick, they performed for a week to overflow-capacity crowds at each concert. Anthony Lund had died a month earlier, and J. Spencer Cornwall was appointed as the Choir's tenth director shortly after their return, on August 26, 1935.

Tabernacle Choir members have usually had good reason to respect the men who have occupied the podium; usually they are held in affection, as well. Few, however, have been as deeply loved as the soft-spoken slender man with the magnificent head of thick, white hair, J. Spencer Cornwall.

Joseph Spencer Cornwall was born on February 23, 1888, in Millcreek, now a suburb of Salt Lake City. He wanted to be a musician from the time he was a very young man. Evan Stephens was a major influence, and Cornwall began his musical studies in Stephens's group singing classes.

"When I was a boy," Cornwall remembers, "Evan Stephens was my idol, and I used to go hear his choir sing. I went to Stephens and asked him if he wouldn't give me some lessons on conducting. So I went down to his home and he went over a great many things, in a completely illogical way. That was his way of doing things. He never had a downbeat. All of Evan Stephens's beats were up. When I got through with my first lesson, he said, 'Well, come back again next week sometime'; he wouldn't indicate a date. I didn't get along with that. But he remained my idol."

Cornwall intended to be an organist, but after studying for several years with John J. McClellan, he discovered that he "had no facility." He initially went into school teaching and had just registered at the University of Utah to study medicine when he met a neighbor, a school superintendent, on a streetcar. Cornwall's friend convinced him to return to music and offered him a job as a music teacher.

Cornwall spent twenty-three years in the school system, eventually becoming supervisor of music for the Salt Lake City public schools. He was also active in community musical affairs as conductor and organizer and each summer directed the Salt Lake Civic Opera in a popular operetta, among which were *Robin Hood*, *The Vagabond King*, and *New Moon*. In 1927, he was invited to conduct the Salt Lake Oratorio Society's Christmas performance of the *Messiah*.

J. Spencer Cornwall

In describing how he became director of the Tabernacle Choir, Cornwall recalls the day Conductor Lund approached him as they were passing each other on the street. "Boy, I'm not well. I don't know how much longer I can continue with the Tabernacle Choir. You'd better get your plate right side up." (At one time it was a Mormon custom to turn one's dinner plate upside down until a prayer had been asked.)

"Well, Tony Lund died in June. I went to my father's place and he said, 'Well, I see Tony has left us. Who's going to be the next Choir director?' And I said: 'Father, I will!' "

In August, Spencer Cornwall received a telephone call from President Heber J. Grant, asking him to come up to his office. When he arrived, President Grant said: "Last night at our meeting we elected you Tabernacle Choir director, what have you got to say about it?" He thought about it for a day, and accepted. "President Grant took me over for the first rehearsal and introduced me. The next morning was the broadcast. I've never known how it went."

Performers are often at the mercy of technicians, and Cornwall had an uncomfortable feeling about the broadcasts, since there was no way to actually hear what was being broadcast. While it was expensive to make an actual recording, Cornwall insisted. What he heard from the recording of the broadcast was a travesty. The KSL engineer had sharply cut the volume on a very loud number, fearing he would blow a tube; the recording engineer had compensated by boosting the volume—and the distortion.

Horrified at the uneven quality of the program, Cornwall insisted that the engineers attend rehearsals and learn to follow sheet music. Further, he urged that the broadcast control room and recording booth be built in the Tabernacle, with the technical work done there instead of at the station. A workable plan was approved, and the sound quality began to improve dramatically. The Tabernacle of the 1970s is itself a giant studio, with the most sophisticated audio, recording, lighting, and video equipment found anywhere.

Cornwall labored quietly and fastidiously to raise the standards of the Choir, to improve their sound as an ensemble. The Choir had had a very limited repertoire—in the 1880s, approximately seventy-five pieces were in active use. Cornwall knew that the Choir needed a large number of pieces to hold the interest of the growing radio audience, and he developed a library of more than 950 compositions, almost 300,000 copies of music.

Today the library includes more than 1,000 individually numbered selections plus a large number of collections, oratorios, and hymnbooks containing perhaps 2,000 more hymns, choruses, and anthems. The music is held in row upon row of mechanized shelving. There is a staff of seven librarians, volunteer Choir members.

At first, Cornwall lacked a strong background in adult choral music repertoire. He studied the publishers' catalogues and diligently read the extensive correspondence which the Choir received each week, much of it from fellow choir directors. "I got help from the criticism, not the compliments." He took pleasure, however, when they supported some of his more controversial programming decisions. He ruffled a lot of feathers, for example, when he first performed a Negro spiritual, but when the favorable mail came in, he "felt rewarded and justified." Listening to the broadcast became a professional duty for choir leaders throughout the country eager to audition and hear new repertoire. For the first time, non-Mormon composers began to write pieces, dedicating them to the Choir, hoping they would get aired. Most are in manuscript; some make it, most don't. Those which do must first have a printing of 400 copies—at the Choir's expense.

Cornwall kept the Choir to an active concert schedule, which included several performances of a staged version of Mendelssohn's *Elijah.* In 1947, the citizens of Utah celebrated the one-hundredth anniversary of the arrival of the first pioneers in the Territory, and Cornwall organized a series of six grand concerts as part of this celebration, featuring some of America's most distinguished singers, including Helen Traubel and Leonard Warren.

Radio continued to be a consuming interest with Maestro Cornwall. He instituted the practice of recording every broadcast for future study, and in 1944, in recognition of the Choir's service to American broadcasting, "Music and the Spoken Word" received the Peabody Award. Around Richard L. Evans's "Spoken Word," Cornwall built a varied program of sacred and secular anthems and oratorio movements, striving for balance of mood and style. He brought the format of the Tabernacle broadcast into the twentieth century, getting away from the opera excerpts and sentimental gospel songs that had been a fairly large part of the Choir's earlier broadcast and concert repertoire, and moving toward music specifically written for a choir in a liturgical setting.

The Choir's finest hour as a broadcast institution under Cornwall's direction came on April 12, 1945, the day Franklin Delano Roosevelt died. A half-hour after his death, executives of the Columbia network called and asked the Choir to perform a memorial broadcast that evening, though they were very concerned that the Choir might not be ready in time. An hour or so later, a vice-president of CBS, Douglas Coulter, called from New York asking how long it would take to get everything in order. An official at KSL told him the Choir was already assembled. "Incredible!" was all he said. The Choir broadcast on 143 stations, its largest audience to that date, performing five numbers for choir and one for organ. It was a Christian, nondenominational program, and a significant example of the level of musicianship the Choir had attained.

The Tabernacle organists, alternating in the daily recital schedule, the weekly broadcasts, and the choir rehearsals, play "live" before hundreds of thousands of visitors in the Tabernacle each year. Their status in the world of organ performers, however, is built upon their broadcasts and recordings. In annual radio polls, Drs. Schreiner and Asper were both voted among the most popular musicians on the air.

Organ playing and organ programming had changed by the 1940s. The Baroque, the golden age of organ music, was being rediscovered, and it was no longer thought that an organ should imitate an orchestra. "The Austin organ was something of a parlor organ," according to Alexander Schreiner. "I said to the Church officials that it was sweet, but we had to have something more heroic. I needed stronger stuff!" With World War II coming to a close, he renewed the appeal. When officials asked him how much it would cost, he replied, "I am merely the organist, not in the finance department." Thirty years later, with a twinkle in his eye, he asks, "Don't you think this was a good answer?" Melvin Dunn, chief organ technician at the Tabernacle, observes, "How Alex ever persuaded the brethren to put a new organ in after thirty years is beyond me, but he did the best thing that ever happened to this Tabernacle."

A contract with Aeolian Skinner Company for a new organ was signed in 1945, at a cost of $90,000, and construction began in 1948. The antiphonal organ relocated from the back wall of the Tabernacle served the recitals and the broadcasts through this period.

G. Donald Harrison, president of Aeolian Skinner, who consulted throughout the construction with Alexander Schreiner, advocated an "American Classic organ," with tonal resources appropriate to virtually every type of music. The Tabernacle organ is a unique instrument and may well be his masterpiece. Today's organ has 11,000 pipes (Ridges's had 2,000) comprising 188 stops. Sitting in the Tabernacle, hearing the organ and the Choir raising their voices to sing the praises of the Lord in the live, warm acoustics, is an aesthetic miracle, an experience to be sought.

In April 1940, America's most famous concert auditorium, Carnegie Hall in New York City, was filled with scientists, patrons of the arts, and newsmen. When the famous curtains were raised, the usual row upon row of performers were nowhere to be seen. The evening was to feature, according to advance accounts, Paul Robeson, Leopold Stokowski and the Philadelphia Orchestra, and last, but by no means least, the Salt Lake Mormon Tabernacle Choir and Organ, conducted by J. Spencer Cornwall. On stage, instead, were large, dark boxes of electronic equipment. It was the first demonstration of a new process: stereophonic, or binaural, recordings developed by a Utah-born scientist, Dr. Harvey Fletcher, working at the Bell Telephone laboratories.

The Choir recording required three tons of equipment, two weeks to set up, and several days to make. Three separate microphones, one for the sopranos at the left, one for the altos at the right, and one for the men's voices in the center, were used. When played back in Carnegie Hall, the spatial relationships were recreated on stage by using separate speakers. With multiple tracks, it was also possible to adjust the balance of one section of the Choir against the others. The age of stereo had begun; the Choir had helped it come into being.

Two Tabernacle Choir recordings, among the first commercial albums recorded expressly for the new long-playing process, were a result of the celebration in 1949 of the Choir's twentieth year of continuous network radio broadcasting. Frank Stanton, president of CBS, suggested that the Choir make two records of favorite compositions from their broadcast repertoire. He further proposed that the profits from these recordings should go to the Choir. With Stanton's

Dimitri Tiomkin, center, explains his musical score for a U.S. Signal Corps film, *Battle of San Pietro,* to Tabernacle organist Frank Asper, left, and conductor J. Spencer Cornwall, right. Looking on is Captain L. D. Evans. Equipment for optical sound track recording was installed in the Tabernacle basement in July 1944.

suggestion began the reliance of the Choir on royalties from recordings for much of their operating budget.

Columbia's team of engineers came to Salt Lake City under the direction of Goddard Lieberson, head of Columbia's Masterwork division. The chief resident engineer in the Tabernacle was Stanley Rees, an immensely inventive and talented technician. Rees had developed a microphone arrangement for the Choir's radio broadcasts which combined several close-in mikes plus an omnidirectional microphone hung at a distance. This arrangement produced good control over the Choir's blend and also picked up enough room resonance. The CBS engineers found Rees's system preferable to their own and adopted it for the first LP recordings. Rees set a tradition which continued in the work of engineer Paul Evans, who in the mid-fifties developed techniques for reproducing the lower tones of the organ and worked tirelessly to improve the fidelity of recordings and broadcasts of the Choir. He feels that the Tabernacle is "one of the toughest places in the world to do a recording, but also one of the loveliest." Columbia's technicians recognized the quality of the work by Rees and his staff and, subsequently, by Evans and his. In organ recordings and Choir numbers requiring only organ accompaniment, entire albums were done solely by the Salt Lake technicians, and forwarded to Columbia for processing.

The first LP featuring the Tabernacle Choir was released on October 24, 1949. It was a ten-inch record (a standard size for the day) called, simply, *The Mormon Tabernacle Choir of Salt Lake City—Volume I.* Volume II, also containing material from the 1949 recording sessions, was released in March 1950. The organist for the first record was Frank Asper; Alexander Schreiner accompanied the second. Both records contained hymns and short oratorio excerpts.

After recording music for several government-sponsored World War II motion picture soundtracks, the Choir's commercial film debut came in 1952, in the first Cinerama release. Cinerama was a wide-screen process utilizing three simultaneously projected images. Lowell Thomas, the news commentator, was producing the film, and to produce an equally spacious sonic effect, he utilized the stereophonic sound system developed by Dr. Fletcher. For the first time, a movie used multichannel sound. The Choir was recorded in six-track stereo in the Tabernacle, and the effect on audiences was staggering, greatly widening the Choir's following.

One of the Choir's long-standing problems was also solved by technology when Dr. Fletcher discovered that the members were not hearing the organ directly—they were hearing its echo bouncing off the back wall. The organ sounds came from behind the singers and passed high over their heads; what they eventually heard was diffused and delayed. Evan Stephens, in his day, had also recognized that the Choir had difficulties hearing the organ, and placed a harmonium player in the Choir seats to double the voice parts. However, this was an unacceptable musical solution, since it destroyed the purity of the choral tone. Dr. Fletcher's solution: use microphones to pick up the organ and then play it back through sixty loudspeakers under the singers' seats. The Choir takes a similar set-up with them when they tour. At a concert in Paris, when no organ was

The Tabernacle Choir during their London tour, singing at the Westminster Cultural Hall

available, Alexander Schreiner played the accompaniment on a grand piano; the sound was piped back to the Choir through twelve speakers. As Cornwall explained the system to a lady choir director, she exclaimed, "Oh, thirteen pianos!"

As the Choir began increasing the number of concerts and tours, and became involved in broadcasting and recording, it was apparent that they would need help in managing the administrative, financial, and logistical details of an expanding program. David A. Smith was the first man appointed to fill this position, serving for thirty years as the President of the Salt Lake Mormon Tabernacle Choir. His administrative and record-keeping abilities, coupled with feelings of endearment toward the individual members, set the pattern for future Choir presidents. In 1938, Salt Lake City businessman Lester F. Hewlett was appointed to succeed Smith in this voluntary position. During Hewlett's administration, the Choir redoubled its recording activities.

The Choir visited seven European countries: Scotland, England, the Netherlands, Denmark, Germany, Switzerland, and France. The singers memorized fifty-seven pieces for the trip, performing in the major concert halls of Glasgow, Manchester, London, Cardiff, Copenhagen, Berlin, Wiesbaden, Amsterdam, Scheveningen, Bern, Zurich, and Paris.

William James once wrote, "The great use of life is to spend it for something that will outlast it." This was one of Cornwall's favorite quotations, and the Choir's recordings were to him a prime example of just that longevity. J. Spencer Cornwall believed strongly that recordings would expand the reputation of the Choir and he never lost his desire to use his Choir to teach the whole world. Cornwall's recordings are filled with the clarity and quiet intelligence which he displayed in all his work. Choir members who sang under him remember him fondly, as a superb musician and a man of good humor. Today's Mormon Tabernacle Choir, known throughout the world by its media exposure and live appearances, was shaped by his vision.

Richard P. Condie

10

Make Haste

RARELY HAD the NBC Television Studios in Burbank seen such an assemblage of the nation's musical talent. They were all there, that November night in 1959: Ella Fitzgerald, Bobby Darin, Jimmy Driftwood, and Frank Sinatra. The occasion: the first annual awards program of the American Academy of Recording Arts and Sciences.

The Grammy Award is the recording industry's equivalent of the movies' Oscar, its symbol a replica of the early mechanical Gramophone, with horn attached to the playback needle and diaphragm. All the artists knew they had won, and the evening was to consist of live performances of the year's most honored recordings. Midway in the program, the studio musicians, filling in for the Philadelphia Orchestra, began the familiar imitation of a slow march beat—*drrrummt . . . , drrrummt . . . , drrrummt, drrrummt, drrrummt*—followed by the muted fanfare of distant trumpets. The doors in an elaborate stage set parted, framing nearly 300 singers clad in blue as Richard P. Condie led them in the words "Mine eyes have seen the glory of the coming of the Lord. . . ."

The Salt Lake Mormon Tabernacle Choir and the Philadelphia Orchestra had been honored by the record industry for an album which featured, among other pieces, "The Battle Hymn of the Republic," which was to become almost as much of a Choir trademark as "Come, Come, Ye Saints." Entered in the vocal group or chorus category, the award was for their collaborative effort under Eugene Ormandy on the Columbia stereo album *The Lord's Prayer.* An additional single release of "The Battle Hymn of the Republic" (backed by the album's title song) quickly made it a favorite of millions who rarely buy a "classical" recording. It was impossible to avoid hearing it several times during a typical day of radio listening, as disc jockeys featured it in their top tune play lists. The success of both recordings indicated the ability of the modern Choir to attract a popular following while performing essentially sacred and classical music.

The years of broadcasting and, now, recordings made the Choir a certain success on any concert tour, anywhere. They had gone on tour a total of twelve times in their first 110 years, culminating in the European tour of 1955. In the next twenty years, they would triple that number of tours, averaging three trips a year.

The amateurs from Salt Lake City performed with the nation's top musicians that night in Burbank, as they had on their hit recording, and in the Academy of Music concerts in Philadelphia; and as they would in future concerts in Cleveland, London, and other cities. They continued to hold the affection of millions of loyal listeners around the world through their broadcasts, which after 1962 would be televised as well.

The new leaders of the Choir, conductor Richard P. Condie and president Isaac M. Stewart, together with organists Alexander Schreiner and Robert Cundick, faced new and exciting opportunities in the age of jet aircraft and the communications satellite.

It would be hard to imagine a greater contrast of personalities and styles than that between J. Spencer Cornwall and his successor, Richard P. Condie. Unlike Cornwall, Condie is an outgoing, highly charged man, the sort who makes everyone in a room feel physically smaller than he or she really is.

Richard Condie was born in 1898 in Springville, Utah. After graduating from the New England Conservatory of Music, he won a scholarship to study voice in Fontainebleau, France, in 1927. Two years later, the young tenor joined a traveling Italian opera company and made his debut in Constantine, Algeria, singing the role of Pinkerton in Puccini's *Madama Butterfly.* He spent some time touring and then returned to New York, where he began to make the rounds—so familiar to young artists—of managers and auditions. Two producers, Schwab and Mandel, liked his work and asked him to try out for the role of Philippe in their hit show *Blue Moon.* On the one hand, there was all the excitement of Broadway and a significant salary—$600 a week—made even more attractive by the fact that the Depression had begun. He was, however, a married man, and his wife, who had been traveling with him, was scheduled to return to Utah to resume her teaching. Half an hour before her departure, Condie also packed his bags. The producers wired him in Salt Lake City that the role was still open. "I turned the offer down," Condie says. "I decided that I would have to make my future here in Utah."

That future included private teaching, singing solos on live radio programs, and producing operas—*Faust* at Utah State Agricultural College and *Hansel and Gretel* at Brigham Young University. Having decided to go into conducting, Condie heard that there was an opening as assistant conductor at the Tabernacle Choir and approached Cornwall, under whom he had sung at the Salt Lake Civic Opera. Cornwall attended music clinics every summer, and that summer he was working with F. Melius Christiansen, the conductor of the famed St. Olaf's Choir. Cornwall suggested Condie come along, and that he might later make him his assistant. Richard Condie recalls, "Conductors from universities and high schools and church choirs were all around. Of course I had very little experience conducting. I had never studied it." But Condie was an apt pupil. When another student asked Christiansen whether anyone there had the potential of being an outstanding choral conductor, the master turned to Condie and said, "Young man, you've got it."

Richard P. Condie was assistant conductor of the Tabernacle Choir for twenty years but conducted few broadcasts. At the same time he held a position at the University of Utah, teaching and conducting.

In 1957, the President of the Church, David O. McKay, asked Condie to be acting conductor of the Choir when Cornwall retired. Condie answered that with such a title he would have no authority. He wanted to be *the* Conductor. President McKay said, "You're too old!" but finally relented and offered him a two-year position. Condie was fifty-nine when he became the eleventh conductor of the Tabernacle Choir and would remain its leader for seventeen years.

Condie's conception of choral tone was sharply different from Cornwall's. While Cornwall was fond of the purity of children's voices, Condie had grown up hearing Italian immigrants singing the romantic old songs and had said to himself, "That's my kind of voice!"

"I heard all the great singers when I was young. They all came to Salt Lake City. I heard Nordica, and Melba, Schumann-Heink, John McCormack. I had all these voices in my mind. So when I went into the Choir, I was not trying to get a straight tone from them; I did want a good blend, but I wanted a sound with warmth and quality—solo quality."

To Condie, the straight tone, the voice without vibrato, was monotonous, "too virtuous." Condie's conducting was based on emotion. "You've got to produce yourself," he would tell the Choir. "Don't try and imitate anybody. Feel this music, speak through it." He was intense and so were his rehearsals.

Condie would begin to work on a piece six weeks before the scheduled broadcast. The first three or four weeks, he would simply read the piece, from beginning to end, without stopping. A week or two before the broadcast, he worked more carefully. On an average rehearsal night the Choir would sing more than twenty compositions.

Condie produced what is often described as "the Tabernacle Choir sound," a great, romantic choral tone, heavy with feeling. It drew added power from the rich sound of the Philadelphia Orchestra, the Choir's recording partner on many projects through the Condie years. Eugene Ormandy says about Condie that "he is a fine conductor and a gentleman—and it is not easy to be a great conductor and a gentleman." Ormandy was pleased by the Choir's sound and its rich blend of textures. He has often stated that "it is the greatest choir in the world."

Richard Condie was aided in his work by Choir president Isaac M. Stewart, a dynamo who sought every opportunity to keep the Choir before the public eye. A retired vice-president and legal counsel of Union Carbide Corporation, Stewart became the third Choir president after the death of his brother-in-law, Lester Hewlett, in 1962. President Stewart brought to his assignment important contacts in the world of business and the arts, and shepherded the Choir through thirteen productive years.

With the combination of Stewart, Richard L. Evans, and Richard P. Condie, the Choir enjoyed a splendid period. An enterprising manager, a beloved commentator, a superior and Romantic conductor, and an economic environment which made frequent touring possible gave the Choir a visibility which it had never enjoyed before.

When Condie left the Choir, Dr. Jay E. Welch, his assistant conductor and successor, wrote an article in *The Tab,* the Choir's newspaper, enumerating the accomplishments of all the previous conductors before concluding, admiringly, "And Richard Condie taught them how to sing."

Some highlights of Condie's seventeen years:

—The Choir's 1962 performance at Mt. Rushmore, transmitted live via Telstar satellite to millions of television viewers in Europe.

—Five World's Fair appearances—in Seattle, 1962; New York City, 1964; Montreal, 1967; San Antonio, 1968; and Spokane, 1974.

—Five trips to the nation's capital, including the inaugurations of presidents Johnson and Nixon, and the national Christmas tree lighting.

—Concert trips to Canada in 1962, 1964, and 1967; to Mexico in 1968 and 1972; and to Europe in 1973, during which the Choir sang in Munich, Paris, and in London, where they made an album for Columbia with the Royal Philharmonic and two television specials for the BBC which are often shown in many parts of the world.

The pattern set by the earliest tours of 1893 and 1911 has remained the norm, despite changes in transportation. Those tours, by rail, in charter trains which became traveling homes, were convenient but too slow by modern standards. When the Choir first took to the air, it took as many as five or six of the propeller-driven planes to handle the job. Now their trips can be handled by one Boeing 747.

Typically, the Choir arrives in a city, has a little time for caravan sight-seeing, rehearses, performs, then gets ready to move to the next city. It may be great fun to go to Europe or to the World's Fairs, but for the Choir, that fun is tied up with a great deal of work.

The Choir often allows the nonsinging spouses of members to travel along (at their own expense). When the Choir party arrives at a hotel, 600 people get off the buses, all checking in at one time, going to dinner together, sight-seeing at the same places. Logistics is the key to any successful Choir trip, and they have become masters at it. But that has come with experience. Their steamship had just left its berth in Montreal for their first European tour in 1955 when an emergency stop was made at Quebec after it became apparent that the ship's supply of milk was woefully inadequate, and that there was going to be a surplus of liquor. And it was a trial for their British hotels to handle 600 guests who did not drink tea.

A Tabernacle Choir tour is like the uprooting and moving of a small town. Since 1893, the Choir has always traveled with a medical staff in attendance, carrying their own medicine and equipment. The dentist on the trip to Europe in 1955 even brought along supplies of emergency dentures and temporary fillings.

An outdoor concert at Marienplatz, Munich

The Choir in Teotíhuacán, Mexico

There have been serious medical problems, and even tragic deaths, on tours. Coming back from Europe in 1955, one singer, a hemophiliac, almost died aboard ship. Without a thought, Choir members with the appropriate blood type gave transfusions, while all joined in fasts and prayer for the unfortunate man. His condition had never been a secret, yet nobody had ever felt it too worrisome to have him as a member of the Choir. He was a brother and valued as a human being, and the other members of the Choir were more than willing to deal with his problem.

Several other Choir members, some traveling with their spouses, took extended sight-seeing tours in Europe after the 1955 concerts ended. Returning home, they were killed less than an hour from home when their plane crashed into a Wyoming mountain peak.

It is precisely its concern for humanity which brings the Choir on tour in the first place. Members tour to present their feelings in music, and singing in the Choir is their contribution to the ongoing development of mankind. The Mormons believe that man's life on earth is a period of growth and testing; the Choir is one of many ways to be constructive and not be overwhelmed by the despair of so much of the world. Touching other people, and developing one's own self: it is a potent combination.

Each year, the Choir receives numerous requests from organizations throughout the world asking for an appearance. The letters come from concert organizers, universities, convention bureaus. The Choir's budget from the Church does not include money for touring, which must be raised independently. The costs of transporting, housing, and feeding 300 people have risen astronomically in the last several years.

Often the Choir is sponsored by a private individual or an organization helping to cover the expenses of some segment of the tour. The organizations are by no means necessarily Mormon. Groups like Rotary and even private insurance firms have sponsored appearances in their cities. They do it because of the good name of the Choir. Corporations and groups in the public interest like to have their names associated with the Choir's and believe that the Choir's appearance is good for the community.

Touring plans are formulated by the president of the Choir in consultation with the General Authorities of the Church. Although the Choir is not a missionary group in the conventional sense—a group about which one could say that it is the cause of many people joining the Church—Church leadership takes a keen interest in its outside activities. It is an organization which creates and maintains good will for the Church and its ideals, which are the cherished possessions of the Choir's members.

Jerold D. Ottley

II

Children of the Promise

WHEN JEROLD OTTLEY was appointed an assistant conductor of the Tabernacle Choir that summer day in 1974, he could hardly have imagined how soon his life would be changed. True, three other assistant conductors had previously ascended to the directorship: Ebenezer Beesley, Richard Condie, and Dr. Jay E. Welch. But if recent experience was any test, it would be years before Ottley might get the nod.

Condie's two decades as assistant to Cornwall had given him only limited public opportunities to conduct. Condie gave his assistant, Jay Welch, regular assignments at General Conferences and in broadcasts. When Welch was appointed director, he continued this practice with Ottley. Six months later, Jay Welch resigned for personal reasons, and Ottley became acting director in December, then director by April 1975.

By the end of that year, virtually an entirely new team was installed at the Tabernacle. Ottley brought in Dr. Donald Ripplinger as assistant conductor, and Dr. John Longhurst became Tabernacle organist in 1977, joining Dr. Robert Cundick, appointed only ten years earlier. J. Spencer Kinard had succeeded Richard L. Evans as commentator in 1972, and Oakley S. Evans was appointed president of the Choir in 1975.

For the first time, the entire music staff were Mormon-born musicians who had earned doctorates in music. They were also younger than any previous team, the luminaries among a large and increasing number of Mormon composers, conductors, and organists in academic and professional music posts in many parts of the United States. The musical heritage of the Mormons was in full flower.

The Choir's thirteenth conductor is soft-spoken and distinguished by a great shock of silver hair and a warm, winning smile. His conducting technique is awesome in its precision. As befits a man who leads an "amateur" choir, he is a superb teacher, devoted to the art of choir building. Dr. Ottley has greatly refined

Jay E. Welch

the Choir's sound and its basic musicianship and expanded its range of repertoire and performance possibilities. His quiet spiritual strength, his outgoing sense of humor, and his dedication to music and to the Church make him an ideal selection.

As a boy, he was an avid trombone player, pushing the slide out with his foot when his arms would not reach. In 1955, after three years as a missionary in New Zealand, he enrolled at Brigham Young University to study music. During his first year of school, he met JoAnn South, a University of Utah music student, and married her a year later. Ottley concentrated on both instrumental and vocal music and, on graduation, taught music in the public schools. He remains committed to education—"I have a bit of chalk dust in my veins," he once remarked —and continues to teach graduate courses at the University of Utah, where in 1967 he earned his master's degree in choral conducting. Having also developed a fine, light tenor voice, he had joined the Tabernacle Choir four years earlier.

Both Ottley and his wife were awarded Fulbright grants in 1968, which enabled them to travel to Cologne, Germany. There he studied German choral conducting practices, while she studied voice. In 1972, he received his doctorate from the University of Oregon and settled comfortably into academic life at the University of Utah.

One of his faculty colleagues was Jay Welch, a dynamic leader with credentials as a composer and conductor, then serving as Richard Condie's assistant. In addition to his duties with the Choir, Dr. Welch organized a group of younger musicians (maximum age, twenty-nine) into the Mormon Youth Symphony and Chorus, who have their own recording, broadcasting, and concert schedule. Many of their experienced singers hope to graduate into the Tabernacle Choir after they "retire." When Welch was appointed director of the Choir in 1975, Ottley readily accepted an invitation from the new conductor to join with another assistant, Dr. Robert Bowden, in working with both the Tabernacle Choir and its "farm club." (Dr. Bowden continues as conductor of the young Mormons.)

Welch's resignation came after a Sunday morning broadcast, and Ottley had to conduct a Christmas concert the next Thursday. Ten years before, as a Choir member who was studying conducting, Ottley heartily—and honestly—denied any ambition to become its director. He had watched the Choir in action, noted all the difficulties and challenges, and decided that the job was the last thing in the world he wanted. And now it was his.

Characteristically, Ottley jumped right in and went to work. His first rehearsal was tense. Conducting an organization like the Mormon Tabernacle Choir involves a great deal more than simply choosing and directing the music. Any excellent performing organization has a very strong awareness of its own worth. But that evening in the middle of the Christmas concert, the Choir members began to relax and have fun doing what they most enjoyed doing. The Choir had rallied behind a new director and has now become devoted to him, respecting his leadership, musicianship, and spirit. A number of today's singers, when asked what they most enjoy about being members of the Mormon Tabernacle Choir answer simply, "Jerry Ottley."

Robert Cundick

The Choir's present assistant conductor, Don Ripplinger, received a degree in music education, taught in the public schools, and earned his master's and doctorate along the way. He taught at the University of Wisconsin at Stevens Point before joining the music faculty at Brigham Young University; a few days later he was appointed associate conductor of the Tabernacle Choir.

Dr. Ripplinger handles many of the musical and personnel functions of the Choir's operations. Much of the joy in his work comes from his association with the Choir members themselves: "It's great to feel the kind of support they give." When Ottley is conducting a rehearsal, Ripplinger serves as his producer—his musical control. A great many details which are hidden by the reverberant haze of the rehearsal hall are ruthlessly exposed by the microphone.

A new position—that of vocal coach—was established by Dr. Ottley, and his wife, JoAnn, assumed this responsibility. An accomplished soloist, she has a beautiful, supple voice, and a firm grasp of technique. Mrs. Ottley devised a series of three workshops, held one week apart, for small groups of singers. Every member attended the series. "I taught basics," she said: breath control, tone production, different styles of singing, and "syllable dissection." Initially, there were worries that the classes were "auditions" designed to weed out weaker members, but the singers soon saw the positive results.

"Singing is basically a deteriorating business," explains Mrs. Ottley. Small errors can creep into the individual voice, and a few people can spread vocal problems throughout a section. The vocal coach continues her work, engaging in what she calls "preventive maintenance." Listening to a tape of the Choir, Dr. Ottley remarked, "The sopranos are getting breathy again. I guess we will have to start working on that once more." JoAnn Ottley knows exactly what the conductor wants.

Dr. Robert Cundick has described his reaction to his appointment as the Tabernacle organist. "I was elated," he said, "for about a week; then the weight of responsibility hit me and has never left." The duties of the Tabernacle organists include not only the Choir accompaniments and daily recitals, but also arranging and even composing for the Choir.

The great organ in the Tabernacle is a splendid instrument. It is a gigantic machine and is equally effective for solo or accompaniment. Cundick says that it is the "easiest large organ to play that I have ever encountered."

Robert Cundick was recommended by Condie and Schreiner to succeed Frank Asper in 1965, and is now the only remaining member of that staff, furnishing continuity and stability during a period of great change.

Born in Salt Lake City on November 26, 1926, Cundick was the first Mormon musician to receive his entire music training to the doctoral level within the Salt Lake Valley, illustrating the remarkable development of music education in Utah. He received his Ph.D. degree in composition in 1955 under Professor Leroy J. Robertson. His principal organ teacher was Alexander Schreiner. He worked his way through school playing jazz piano in dance bands (sometimes sitting opposite trombonist Jerold Ottley), serving as organist for the First Unitarian Church and

John Longhurst

Temple B'nai Israel, and teaching numerous private students. Upon graduation, he turned to teaching at Brigham Young University.

Church President David O. McKay called him at age thirty-four to serve as organist for the Church's striking new Hyde Park Chapel in London. "The best part of the experience was the opportunity to have two years alone in a very exciting and vital musical environment. It shaped my own musical aesthetic." A year after his return to Utah he was named Tabernacle organist.

Cundick won the American Guild of Organists' S. Lewis Elmer Award for the highest score in professional degree examinations two consecutive years. He is a Fellow and former national councilor of the Guild.

John Longhurst is a tall, noticeably erect man, in contrast to Bob's short, somewhat scholarly appearance. He was born in Placerville, California, June 23, 1940, then moved with his family to Utah at an early age. He received his bachelor's degree from the University of Utah and his Doctor of Musical Arts degree from Eastman School of Music. He has studied with Alexander Schreiner, David Craighead, and Robert Noehren. After graduation in 1969, he taught at Brigham Young University until 1978, when he was called to be a Tabernacle organist. Longhurst is also a Fellow of the American Guild of Organists.

When asked how long it took for him to learn to play the Tabernacle organ, he answers with two statements. "Well, it didn't take very long to play it at all—one who has had an organ background knows what to do with an instrument to begin with. The other answer is that we are still learning to use the organ—the combination of stops is almost limitless. Fifty years from now I'll still be learning to play this organ."

This is the kind of man John Longhurst is: direct, honest, without frills. His playing reflects the same strengths.

Cundick and Longhurst operate as a team, rather than as artistic competitors. When one is at the organ console, the other is in the audio or video booth evaluating the performance and communicating the results by intercom. It is not uncommon during rehearsal for the "booth organist" to dash to the console and change organ stops to alter the tone color which is being picked up by the microphones. On occasion, they will accompany the Choir as an organ duo, or include other instruments in addition. Neither hesitates to use the piano when it is better suited to the accompaniment. On tour, when an adequate organ is not available, they often collaborate in piano duo accompaniments.

"One never knows what to expect with those two," Ottley grins, "but one thing is certain—the results will be both musically exciting and perfectly valid every time. They are a great source of strength, both musically and spiritually, for the Choir."

John Longhurst is optimistic about the future of the Choir.

"As our national life becomes more profane, those who appreciate what we are trying to do will remain committed to maintaining a standard of excellence."

A third Tabernacle organist, Roy M. Darley, alternates with Cundick and Longhurst for the recitals and accompanies the Mormon Youth Chorus. He also plays on the Choir broadcasts several times each year.

J. Spencer Kinard

Following the death of Richard L. Evans, the Choir's commentator for forty-one years, the assignment went to another young Mormon who, like Evans, was then working for KSL, but in television news.

J. Spencer Kinard joined the news department of KSL-Television in 1965. Three years later he was awarded a CBS Fellowship to study at Columbia University. CBS then hired him as a writer for their radio network, and, after several years there, his career was zooming. "I realized that my life had reached something of a crossroads," he recalls. But he saw little prospect of a job in television at CBS, and so he called KSL, who told him they had a job if he wanted it. He decided to move back to Salt Lake City, then only the forty-fourth largest TV market area in the nation. Though his media friends thought he was giving up an excellent career, he resumed work at KSL-TV as a television newscaster.

A year later, almost to the day he left New York, J. Spencer Kinard became the commentator of "Music and the Spoken Word." When Evans died, Kinard was KSL's Church reporter. But though he soon knew who was going to replace Evans, he wouldn't be able to report his scoop.

Kinard was invited to audition for the Choir position and to prepare several "Spoken Word" messages on videotape. Knowing all the technicians, he was unafraid when he made the tapes. But he was deeply humbled—even scared—when he learned he had been selected.

Kinard likes to draw from his newscaster's background as he deals with contemporary problems, but his "Spoken Word" messages are written in the pattern developed by Richard L. Evans. Though not a high Church official, as Evans was, Kinard holds a position of great responsibility: as commentator of the Tabernacle Choir broadcasts he is the Latter-day Saint whose voice and appearance are most recognized by people outside the Church.

Oakley S. Evans is an energetic Salt Lake City business executive. In 1975, the First Presidency of the Church selected him as president of the Choir; characteristically, Oakley Evans accepted the call. After spending the summer working with the retiring president, Isaac Stewart, he officially assumed his post in September.

As a student he had played piano, trumpet, and especially the bass fiddle, and at Brigham Young University he had performed in a quartet with a man who was to become one of Utah's most renowned composers, Dr. Leroy J. Robertson. "Then I went into business," says President Evans, "and that was the end of my musical instruments."

Oakley Evans was a senior executive of the J. C. Penney Corporation when he retired, just before assuming the presidency of the Choir. But Evans didn't stay retired very long, accepting the position as president of ZCMI—Zion's Cooperative Mercantile Institution—the oldest incorporated department store in America. He works a full day at ZCMI, then often spends as much time after hours on Choir business.

The presidency of the Choir is a voluntary, unpaid job. Only the conductor, the Choir's two organists, and a secretary receive full-time salaries; the assistant conductor is a part-time salaried appointment. The Choir's organization, however, includes a small army of forty members who have, in addition, shouldered administrative tasks. Except for the salaries, the Choir pays its own expenses, primarily through royalties from the sale of records and concert ticket sales.

In consultation with the conductor and the officials of Columbia Records, President Evans plans and directs the Choir's recordings. He works tirelessly to expand the Choir's market and to develop its audience. He is also investigating new and more creative uses of the broadcast media, so that the Choir will be before the public eye in the best possible light.

Developing concert tours is another of his duties, deciding when and where the Choir will go and directing the appropriate fund-raising activities. Evans is responsible to the General Authorities of the Church, with whom he frequently consults. Transcending his executive role is President Evans's evident love and respect for the organization he serves. He is always available to its members to discuss any problem or share any joy. His warmth is communicated to the Choir in his weekly announcements.

Evans is aided in his work by Udell Poulsen, the business manager of the Choir. Another volunteer, Poulsen handles the financial details of the Choir's operation, a difficult task which he approaches with dedication and dry humor.

A COLLECTION OF

HYMNS AND ANTHEMS,

SET TO MUSIC BY HOME COMPOSERS.

———— ❧ ————

RESPECTFULLY COMPILED BY
CHARLES JEFFREY CALMAN
FOR YOUR EDIFICATION AND DELIGHT.

FOR THE USE OF THE

SALT LAKE CITY TABERNACLE CHOIR

Or FOR GATHERINGS BY THE HEARTH.

———— ❧ ————

SALT LAKE CITY, UTAH.

THE MUSIC of the Mormons is a building block of their history and an important aspect of their Choir. Included in this section are fourteen hymns and anthems, some written especially for the Choir, some illustrating events of historical importance, some composed by conductors of the Choir or Tabernacle organists. All of them are associated with the Choir's repertoire; all are popular favorites.

The selections are arranged in the form of an extended Mormon Tabernacle Choir broadcast, the only unusual circumstance being that all the compositions are by Mormon composers. The programming offers a variety of contrasting moods and styles. This section of the book is intended for your use, for you and your family to play at the piano, or sing by the fire. It is hoped that you will find this an enjoyable experience and another insight into the nature of the Tabernacle Choir.

The collection opens with Thomas Griggs's "Gently Raise the Sacred Strain," which has opened the Choir broadcasts for more than forty of its fifty years. "Come, Come, Ye Saints," by William Clayton, is the most famous of all Mormon hymns. "The Spirit of God Like a Fire Is Burning" was composed by William W. Phelps and used for the dedication of the Kirtland Temple. It shows the sturdy, rousing style of much of the early Mormon music. "The Morning Breaks, the Shadows Flee" was composed by George Careless, the Choir's sixth conductor. The words are by Parley Pratt and appeared in 1840 on the first page of the first edition of the *Millenial Star,* the publication of the Mormons in Great Britain. Careless's successor was Ebenezer Beesley; his "High on the Mountain Top" appears next. The text is an expression of Isaiah's prophecy "And it shall come to pass, in the last days, that the mountain of the Lord's house shall be exalted above the hills, and all nations shall flow unto it" (Isaiah 2:2). Another mountain piece is Evan Stephens's grand anthem, "Let the Mountains Shout for Joy." This is as fine an example of Stephens's muscular, joyous style as one could desire. The centerpiece of this group of pieces is Leroy Robertson's setting of "The Lord's Prayer." Robertson was one of the finest composers that Utah has produced. This piece is a movement of his *Book of Mormon Oratorio,* written for the Mormon Tabernacle Choir. The entire oratorio (including this section) was based on a chorale tune. Dr. Robertson, when teaching composition or theory, liked to give his students this chorale to harmonize as a classroom exercise. One day, when a student asked him what he could do with it, the professor wrote a harmonization on the blackboard. A few minutes later when all the students had left, Dr. Robertson looked at what he had written in the inspiration of the moment, took a pencil, and copied it down on a sheet of music paper. That blackboard exercise was "The Lord's Prayer." It is the most difficult piece presented in this section, but with some practice (and a listen or two to the Choir's recording) should not prove so hard after all. "O My Father" is a change of pace, one of the most beautiful tunes in the entire Latter-day Saints' repertoire, with an exquisite accompanying text. "I Need Thee Every Hour," by Robert Lowry, with text by Annie S. Hawkes, is an enormously popular hymn with the Choir and with congregations throughout the Church. It is a personal hymn, with the individual speaking to God. Next come hymns by three of the Tabernacle organists. John J. McClellan's "Sweet Is the Work, My God, My King" is commonly performed by the Choir and in the Church. It is a solid, forthright piece of work, easy to play and sing. Alexander Schreiner's "Thy Spirit, Lord, Has Stirred Our Souls" is an excellent example of his style, which was influenced by the German chorale. Robert Cundick's "Easter Morn" represents his attempts to combine a contemporary idiom of composition with a simple style. It also shows his attention to the needs of the amateur musician, for it is very easy to play and sing. Cundick is getting away from the "choir" style which has been so prevalent in Mormon music for nearly the last century and is writing with the capabilities of the congregation in mind.

We conclude our broadcast, as all broadcasts conclude, with "As the Dew from Heaven Distilling." It is always performed on the organ, but it is perfectly singable; try it once just to learn the words. After each broadcast, and at the end of every concert, the Choir sings to the audience "God Be with You 'Till We Meet Again." It can be the most moving moment of any Choir performance.

Please turn the page—and *sing.*

Gently Raise the Sacred Strain

Words by William W. Phelps

Music by Thomas C. Griggs

1. Gent - ly raise the sa - cred strain,
2. Ho - ly day, de - void of strife;
3. Sweet - ly swells the sol - emn sound

For the Sab - bath's come a - gain That man may
Let us seek e - ter - nal life That great re -
While we bring our gifts a - round Of bro - ken

rest, That man may rest, And re - turn his thanks to
ward, That great re - ward, And par - take the sac - ra -
hearts, Of bro - ken hearts, As a will - ing sac - ri -

God, — For his bless - ings — to the blest,
ment — In re - mem - brance — of our Lord,
fice, — Show -ing what — his — grace im - parts,

For — his — bless - ings to the blest.
In — re - mem - brance of our Lord.
Show - ing — what his grace im - parts.

4. Happy type of things to come,
   When the Saints are gathered home
   To praise the Lord,
   In eternity of bliss,
   All as one with sweet accord.

5. Holy, holy is the Lord;
   Precious, precious is his word;
   Repent and live;
   Though your sins be crimson red,
   Oh, repent, and he'll forgive.

6. Softly sing the joyful lay,
   For the Saints to fast and pray!
   As God ordains,
   For his goodness and his love,
   While the Sabbath day remains.

Come, Come, Ye Saints

Words by William Clayton

English Folk Tune

1. Come, come ye Saints, no toil nor la - bor fear; But with joy
2. Why should we mourn or think our lot is hard? 'Tis not so;

wend your way. Though hard to you this jour - ney may ap - pear,
all is right. Why should we think to earn a great re - ward,

Grace shall be as your day. 'Tis __ bet - ter far __ for
If we now shun the fight? Gird __ up your loins; __ fresh

us to strive— Our use - less cares— from us to drive; Do
cour - age take;— Our God will nev - er us for - sake; And

this and joy your heart will swell—All is well! all is well!
soon we'll have this tale to tell— All is well! all is well!

3. We'll find the place which God for us prepared,
   Far away in the West,
   Where none shall come to hurt or make afraid;
   There the Saints will be blessed.
   We'll make the air with music ring,
   Shout praises to our God and King;
   Above the rest these words we'll tell—
   All is well! all is well!

4. And should we die before our journey's through,
   Happy day! all is well!
   We then are free from toil and sorrow, too;
   With the just we shall dwell!
   But if our lives are spared again
   To see the Saints their rest obtain,
   O how we'll make this chorus swell—
   All is well! all is well!

The Spirit of God

Words by William W. Phelps

1. The Spir - it of God like a fire ___ is burn - ing! The lat - ter - day glo - ry be - gins ___ to come forth; The vi - sions and
2. The Lord is ex - tend - ing the Saints' un - der stand - ing, Re - stor - ing their judg - es and all ___ as at first. The knowl - edge and

bless - ings of old are re - turn - ing, And
pow - er of God are ex - pand - ing, The

an - gels are com - ing to vis - it the earth. We'll
veil — o'er the earth — is be - gin - ning to burst.

sing and we'll shout with the ar - mies of

heav - en, — Ho - san - na, ho - san - na to

God   and   the   Lamb!   Let   glo -   ry   to

them   in   the   high -   est   be   giv -   en,   Hence -

forth   and   for -   ev -   er;   A - men   and   a - men!

3. We'll call in our solemn assemblies in spirit,
To spread forth the kingdom of heaven abroad,
That we through our faith may begin to inherit
The visions and blessings and glories of God.

4. How blessed the day when the lamb and the lion
Shall lie down together without any ire,
And Ephraim be crowned with his blessing in Zion,
As Jesus descends with his chariot of fire!

The Morning Breaks

Words by Parley P. Pratt

Music by George Careless

1. The morn - ing breaks; the shad - ows flee; ——
2. The clouds of er - ror dis - ap - pear ——

Lo, Zi - on's stan - dard —— is —— un - furled! The
Be - fore the rays —— of —— truth —— di - vine; The

dawn - ing —— of a bright - er —— day, The
glo - ry —— burst - ing from —— a - far, The

dawn - ing___ of a___ brigh - ter___ day Ma -
glo - ry___ burst - ing___ from___ a - far Wide

jes - tic___ ris - es___ on the world.
o'er the___ na - tions___ soon will shine.

3. The Gentile fulness now comes in,
   And Israel's blessings are at hand.
   Lo, Judah's remnant, cleansed from sin,
   Lo, Judah's remnant, cleansed from sin,
   Shall in their promised Canaan stand.

4. Jehovah speaks! let earth give ear,
   And Gentile nations turn and live.
   His mighty arm is making bare,
   His mighty arm is making bare
   His covenant people to receive.

5. Angels from heaven and truth from earth
   Have met, and both have record borne;
   Thus Zion's light is bursting forth,
   Thus Zion's light is bursting forth,
   To bring her ransomed children home.

High on the Mountain Top

Words by Joel H. Johnson

Music by Ebenezer Beesley

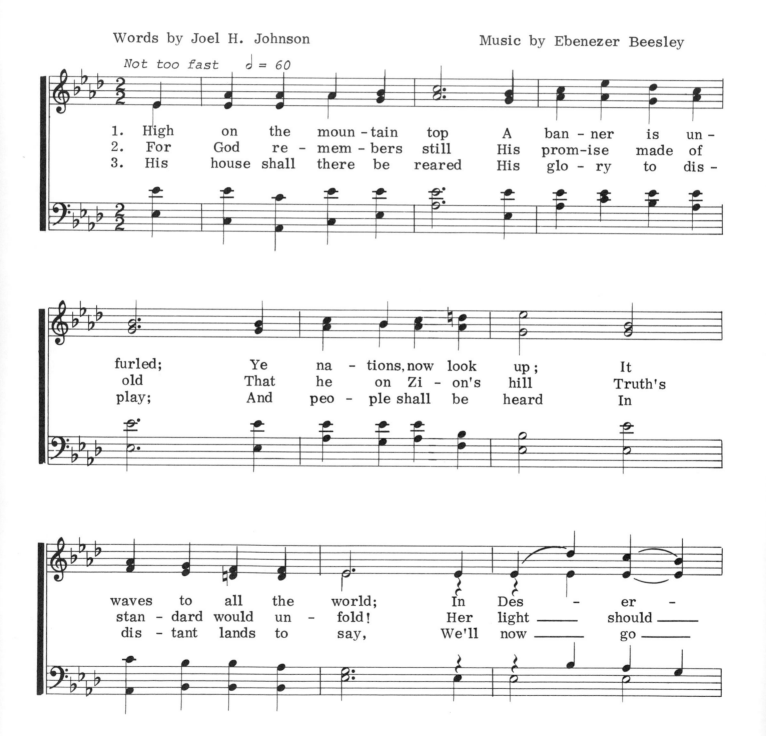

1. High on the moun-tain top A ban - ner is un-furled; Ye na - tions, now look up; It waves to all the world; In Des - er-
2. For God re - mem - bers still His prom-ise made of old That he on Zi - on's hill Truth's stan - dard would un - fold! Her light should
3. His house shall there be reared His glo - ry to dis-play; And peo - ple shall be heard In dis - tant lands to say, We'll now go

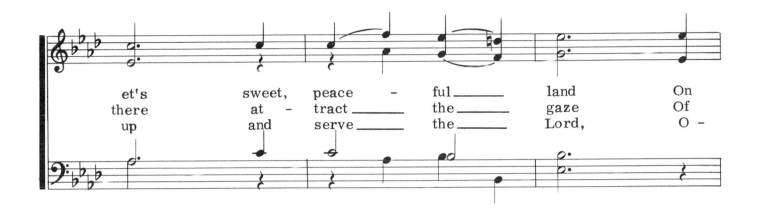

et's sweet, peace - ful_____ land On
there at - tract_____ the_____ gaze Of
up and serve_____ the_____ Lord, O -

Zi - on's mount_____ be - hold it stand!
all the world_____ in lat - ter days.
bey his truth_____ and learn his word.

4. For there we shall be taught
 The law that will go forth,
 With truth and wisdom fraught,
 To govern all the earth;
 Forever there his ways we'll tread,
 And save ourselves with all our dead.

5. Then hail to Deseret!
 A refuge for the good,
 And safety for the great,
 If they but understood
 That God with plagues will shake
  the world
 Till all its thrones shall down be
  hurled.

6. In Deseret doth truth
 Rear up its royal head;
 Though nations may oppose,
 Still wider it shall spread;
 Yes, truth and justice, love and grace,
 In Deseret find ample place.

Let the Mountains Shout for Joy

Evan Stephens

joy ———— and —— glad-ness now are found ——— there -

joy and glad - ness now are found there -

joy and glad - ness now are found there -

in —— thanks-giv-ing and the voice of mel - o - dy, thanks-

in thanks-giv-ing and the voice of —— mel - o - dy, thanks-

giv - ing and the voice＿＿ of＿ mel - o - dy, thanks-

giv - ing and the voice＿＿ of＿ mel - o - dy, thanks-

giv - ing and the voice of mel - o - dy.

giv - ing and the voice of mel - o - dy.

141

The Lord's Prayer

Adagio

Leroy Robertson

done,— Thy King-dom come Thy will be done on earth as it is in

done,— Thy King -dom come Thy will be done on earth as it is in

done,— Thy King-dom come Thy will be done on earth as it is in

done,— And Thy will be done on earth as it is in

heav'n, on — earth as it is in heav'n. Give us this day our dai - ly

heav'n, on — earth as it is — in heav'n. Give us this day our dai - ly

heav'n, on — earth as it — is in heav'n. Give us this day our dai - ly

heav'n, on — earth as it is in heav'n. Give us this day our dai - ly

bread and for - give us our debts as we for - give our deb - tors

bread and for - give us our debts as we for - give our deb - tors

bread and for - give us our debts as we for - give our deb - tors

bread and for - give us our debts as we for - give our deb - tors

and lead us not in - to temp - ta - tion but de -

and lead us not in - to temp - ta - tion but de -

and lead us not in - to temp - ta - tion but de -

and lead us not in - to temp - ta - tion but de -

pow - er, The pow'r and the glo - ry,_____ For

pow - er, The pow'r and the glo - ry,_____ For

pow - er, The pow'r and the glo - ry,_____ For

pow - er, The pow'r and the glo - ry,_____ For

ev - er, For - ev - er and ev - er, A -

ev - er, For - ev - er and ev - er, A -

ev - er, For - ev - er and ev - er, A -

ev - er, For - ev - er and ev - er, A -

men, A -

men, A -

men, A -

men, A -

men, For - ev - er A - men.

men, For - ev - er A - men.

men, For - ev - er A - men.

men, For - ev - er A - men.

O My Father

Words by Eliza R. Snow

Music by James McGranahan

With contemplation ♩.=42

1. O___ my Fa - ther, thou___ that dwell - est In___ the
2. For___ a wise and glo - rious pur - pose Thou___ hast

high_____ and glo - rious place,_____ When___ shall
placed_____ me here___ on earth,_____ And___ with -

I re - gain___ thy pres - ence, And a - gain___ be-hold___ thy
held the rec - ol - lec - tion Of___ my form - er friends___ and

face?___ In ___ thy ho - ly hab - i - ta - tion, Did ___ my
birth,___ Yet ___ oft-times ___ a se - cret some-thing Whis - pered,

In thy ho-ly hab - i - ta - tion,

spir - it once ___ re - side? ___ In ___ my first ___ pri - me - val
"You're ___ a stran-ger here;" ___ And ___ I felt ___ that I ___ had

Did my spir-it once ___ re - side? In my first pri-me - val

child - hood, Was ___ I nur - tured near thy side? _____
wan - dered From ___ a more ___ ex - alt - ed sphere. _____

child - hood, Was I nur-tured near thy side?

3. I had learned to call thee Father,
   Through thy Spirit from on high;
   But until the key of knowledge
   Was restored, I knew not why.
   In the heavens are parents single?
   No; the thought makes reason stare!
   Truth is reason, truth eternal
   Tells me I've a mother there.

4. When I leave this frail existence,
   When I lay this mortal by,
   Father, Mother, may I meet you
   In your royal courts on high?
   Then, at length, when I've completed
   All you sent me forth to do,
   With your mutual approbation
   Let me come and dwell with you.

I Need Thee Every Hour

Words by Annie S. Hawkes

Music by Robert Lowry

1. I need thee ev-ery hour, Most gra - cious Lord; No ten - der voice like thine Can peace af - ford.
2. I need thee ev-ery hour, Stay thou near - by; Temp-ta - tions lose their power When thou art nigh. I need thee; O I need thee;

Ev - ery hour I need thee! O bless me now, my

Sav - ior; I come _____ to thee!

3. I need thee every hour,
In joy or pain;
Come quickly and abide,
Or life is vain.

4. I need thee every hour,
Most Holy One;
O make me thine indeed,
Thou blessed Son!

Sweet Is the Work

Words by Isaac Watts

Music by Ebenezer Beesley

1. Sweet is the work, my God, my King,
2. Sweet is the day of sa - cred rest.
3. My heart shall tri - umph in my Lord

To praise thy name, give thanks and sing,
No mor - tal care shall seize my breast.
And bless his works and bless his word.

To show thy love by morn - ing light
O may my heart in tune be found
Thy works of grace, how bright they shine!

And talk of all thy truths___ at night.
Like Da - vid's harp of sol - emn sound!
How deep thy coun - sels, how ___ di - vine!

4. But, oh, what triumph shall I raise
   To thy dear name through endless days,
   When in the realms of joy I see
   Thy face in full felicity.

5. Sin, my worst enemy before,
   Shall vex my eyes and ears no more.
   My inward foes shall all be slain
   Nor Satan break my peace again.

6. Then shall I see and hear and know
   All I desired and wished below,
   And every power find sweet employ
   In that eternal world of joy.

Thy Spirit, Lord, Has Stirred Our Souls

Words by Frank I. Kooyman

Music by Alexander Schreiner

1. Thy Spir - it, Lord, has stirred our souls, And by its
2. "Did not our hearts with - in us burn?" We know the

in - ward shin - ing glow We see a - new our sa - cred
Spir - it's fire is here. It makes our souls for ser - vice

goals And feel thy near - ness here be - low. No burn - ing
yearn; It makes the path of du - ty___ clear. Lord, may it

bush near Si - na - i Could show thy pres - ence, Lord, more nigh.
prompt us, day by day, In all we do, in all we say.

That Easter Morn

Words by Marion D. Hanks

Music by Robert Cundick

1. That East-er morn a grave___ that burst Pro-claimed to man that
2. This morn re-news for us___ that day When Je-sus cast the
3. Thus we in grat-i-tude___ re-call And give our love and

"Last and First" Had ris'n a-gain___ And con-quered
bonds a-way, Took liv-ing breath___ And con-quered
pledge our all, Shed grate-ful tear___ And con-quer

pain.___

death.___

fear.

As the Dew from Heaven Distilling

Words by Parley P. Pratt

Music by Joseph J. Daynes

1. As the dew from heaven distilling
2. Let thy doctrine, Lord, so gracious,

Gently on the grass descends
Thus descending from above,

And revives it, thus fulfilling
Blest by thee, prove efficacious

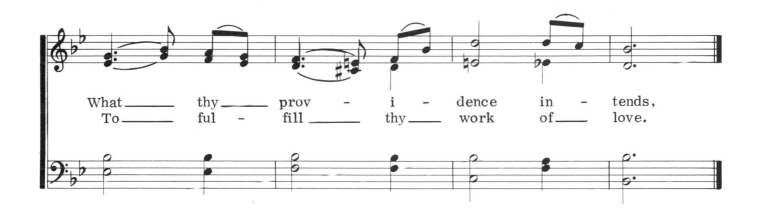

What___ thy___ prov - i - dence in - tends,
To___ ful - fill ___ thy___ work of ___ love.

3. Lord, behold this congregation;
   Precious promises fulfill;
   From thy holy habitation
   Let the dews of life distil.

4. Let our cry come up before thee;
   Thy sweet Spirit shed around,
   So the people shall adore thee
   And confess the joyful sound.

God Be with You Till We Meet Again

Words by J.E. Rankin

Music by W.G. Tomer

The Fitzgerald family at home making music.

12

Make a Joyful Noise

WHEN JUDITH ANNE SPENDLOVE was eleven, she sang in a large primary-children's chorus in the Salt Lake Tabernacle, and from that time dreamed of becoming a member of the Tabernacle Choir. Her hopes dimmed when her family moved away from Utah and she married a native of Washington, with whom she had five children. But then her husband took a new job in Utah, and they both applied for Choir membership. "We never quite faced up to what we would do if only one of us was successful," she declared. Her dream of twenty-six years became a reality when she and her husband, Michael Fitzgerald, were introduced to the Choir with six other new members.

Within weeks of their arrival in their new home in West Jordan, they began an initiation process every modern Choir member must pass through, a process that takes two months to complete. During this time, the couple had to readjust to the demands of their new responsibilities—the excitement still shows in their faces—and their children took on added duties at home to make their parents' membership possible.

It was once a much simpler matter. Mary Jack, the Choir's secretary emeritus at age eighty, recalls what being accepted into the Choir was like under Evan Stephens sixty years ago. She approached director Stephens, who acknowledged that there were some empty seats in the women's section—and that was it. Her only requirement: a desire to join. "I continued in the Choir under Professor Anthony C. Lund. They seemed not to be so particular in that day about auditions or I never could have made it," she declares. "Brother J. Spencer Cornwall was more particular about auditions, and I expected to be turned down, but he let me sing. I asked him one day how come he let me in the Choir, and he said, 'I wanted a secretary.'"

Choir membership was almost lifelong for singers like Ken Rogerson and Jessie Evans Smith, both of whom were members for fifty-three years. Some

singers were admitted while still in their teens, and many continued singing until they were well into their seventies. But while the singer may continue to be willing, the voice may, with other elements of the flesh, weaken. To recruit singers during their most effective years and also to avoid the painful day when a dedicated veteran singer must be unwillingly released, Oakley Evans and Jerold Ottley are implementing new guidelines which have dramatically changed the age difference among Choir members.

The minimum age for new Choir applicants is thirty, and retirement is automatic at sixty, or after twenty years of service, whichever comes first. A few youngsters of twenty-six and a few senior citizens up to sixty-three are still in the Choir, but only during a transition period. The most common age of members is 50.

Craig Fairbanks, a thirty-one-year-old general contractor, became one of the first of a new crop of well-trained young singers to be accepted in the Choir under the new minimum-age rule. He joined the baritone section after five years of singing in the Mormon Youth Chorus, from which he retired when he turned thirty. Young Fairbanks was also continuing a family tradition, being the third generation of Tabernacle Choir members, following his mother and grandfather.

Present day applicants are competing with hundreds of aspiring singers and must meet a stringent set of requirements. The Choir is attempting more and more difficult music, and under very real time constraints; Jerold Ottley and his musical staff require competent musicians, not just shower sopranos and barbershop baritones. A musical balance between sections must also be preserved. Excellent baritones are not even auditioned if that section is already filled, yet a less talented low-bass might get a hearing if there were several anticipated vacancies.

Every three months, new aspirants are screened. An application form starts the process and also spells out the obligations. Television makes physical appearance a factor; obesity has kept talented singers out. Applicants must also obtain a letter of recommendation from the bishop of their local congregation certifying that they meet the moral and spiritual standards required of all Church officers, and that heavy commitment to the Choir will not be detrimental to them or their families.

If the Choir's anticipated vacancies match the applicant's voice range, an audition recording is requested and reviewed, followed by the toughest test yet, a written fundamentals of music examination. A score of eighty-five percent is passing, below fifty percent is not; a score in between is "provisional" and tutoring may be necessary, even after the singer is accepted. The exam was administered to all members of the Choir and many took a series of classes to prepare for it. Typically, members extended themselves to help each other; eventually, all passed. Sight-reading ability improved immensely. "They can do things now that would have been unthinkable two years ago," Dr. Ottley observed.

The final hurdle is an appearance before the audition committee: director, assistant director, vocal coach, and one of the Choir's section leaders who sits in, in a nonvoting capacity, to monitor the audition. The singer demonstrates his vocal range, sight-reading ability, and his confidence in singing his part on one line of a hymn while Ottley sings a distracting pattern. A week later, a letter from the Choir officers announces the results. When the Fitzgeralds both were accepted, they were reminded of their commitments of time, effort, exemplary living, and maintaining good health. In addition, Tabernacle Choir members are encouraged in their other Church obligations, and are told that Choir membership does not excuse them from other responsibilities to Church and, especially, to family.

The Fitzgeralds took the counsel to heart. He is conductor of the local church choir. As president of the Women's Relief Society, she holds the most important position of leadership among the women. Special preparations are made Saturday so that food, clothing, the children's hair, and the family automobiles are all ready for Sunday morning. A baby-sitter takes care of Rebecca and Rachel, six-year-old twins, and two-year-old Katie, while Michael, sixteen, and Daniel, fifteen, attend the morning Priesthood meeting. When the older brothers return home, they make sure their sisters are ready for Sunday School and take turns carrying Katie to their classes—diapers, bottle, and all.

The group of incoming Choir members attends an orientation meeting with the Choir president and members of the staff, and then are measured for Choir costumes by the women's and men's dress committees. After being introduced to the Choir members, they attend rehearsals for two weeks and observe the broadcasts from the audience before finally taking their places, in costume, for their first broadcast.

The men have four basic outfits: black and medium blue suits and light blue and rust-colored jackets with black trousers. Accessories include white and gold shirts and five ties, three cravats and two bows. Women, however, are issued six outfits and a total of fourteen items of apparel. Two formal gowns, in white and rose, are reserved for concerts, while the broadcasts require black skirts with gold or copper blouses, a blue tailored suit, and a two-piece long dress in light blue.

Once admitted, every Choir member is expected to maintain high musical standards, and a constant reauditioning is taking place during rehearsals. A high-fidelity cassette recorder is passed along assigned rows of singers. Each person turns on the recorder, identifies himself, and then proceeds with the rehearsal for approximately three minutes. The tape gives the musical staff a good idea of how well the singer reads his part, responds to instructions, and blends with other voices.

The singers must also maintain the moral standards of the Church and follow the dietary code, the Word of Wisdom, which among other things forbids the use of tobacco, alcohol, and "hot beverages" (meaning coffee and tea).

"Togetherness" has a special meaning for the Fitzgeralds and the thirty-five other married couples who make up twenty-three percent of the Choir. Nine of every ten members are married, and collectively they are the parents of 1,200 children. As one person said, "It may have a giant sound, but it is just a big bunch of mommies and daddies!"

One of every ten members has had a parent in the Choir, and one of every thirty, a grandparent. Several families have been represented by three generations. Strong links to earlier Choir years are altos Susan Cook and Janice B. Hartvigsen, direct descendants of former Choir directors John Parry and Ebenezer Beesley, respectively.

When Lloyd Neal's thirty years as a member of the Choir end with his retirement in 1981, he will have had the satisfaction of seeing two sons, Richard and David, accepted as Choir members.

Not only is the Choir made up of representatives of large families, it is a large family in itself. Its members love to get together socially, and the Choir is famous for its parties: 300 performers in one room each trying to out-ham the others. The Choir is not a collection of individuals whose affection for each other stops at the Tabernacle door.

A dozen committees made up mostly of singing members keep the complex organization functioning smoothly. There are nine members on the library committee, five on transportation, three on activities, a ladies' dress committee of seven, and a one-man dress committee for men, a coordinator for record sales, three secretaries, an historian, an editor, and a social services committee of five. When death claims a member or former member, it is not unusual for a group of Choir members, often directed by Ottley or Ripplinger, to provide choral music for the funeral. Remembrances at times of birth, illnesses, and anniversaries are common, continuing the fraternalism initiated in Ebenezer Beesley's day.

Small wonder, then, that leaving the Choir can be difficult. The new twenty-year retirement rule was presented to Choir members during a special meeting where they recognized, despite personal regrets, its fairness and benefits. Local Church congregations benefit by the return of dedicated, experienced people from the Choir, former Choir members have new opportunities for volunteer service to the Church and community, and more singers have the opportunity to participate. One former member felt guilty about being in the Choir for so long and "hogging the opportunity." After taking a month's leave to care for his ailing mother, he returned to the Tabernacle for a farewell visit. Steeling himself to announce his resignation, he was met by a large group of friends, including Jerold Ottley, who inquired about his mother and told him they were glad to see him back. He found it impossible to bring himself to resign, and is now relieved that his retirement date was set for him by official policy.

"Where on earth do the Mormons find so many admirable voices?" a Philadelphia music critic once wrote after a Choir concert. Two-thirds of them were born in Utah, one-fourth come from other states; and the remaining members are foreign-born. In addition, the large majority, eighty-six percent, are Mormon-born, the remaining fourteen percent are converts. Thus, approximately nine of every ten Choir members are products of the Mormon society and a reflection of its emphasis on culture and learning.

The members' credentials demonstrate that they are remarkably well educated and cosmopolitan, especially for a volunteer "amateur" choir. More than half are college graduates, with one in four having also done graduate work. One-fifth of those singing in the Choir received college degrees in music; among the women the ratio is one in four. Many others chose music as their minor subject.

Almost half of the singers are familiar with one or more foreign languages, especially German, Spanish, and French, but also including Hebrew, Romanian, Finnish, Afrikaans, Maori, Czech, and Tongan. Eighty-five Choir members have served their Church as full-time missionaries, more than fifty of them outside the United States. Thirty six of the seventy-one tenors have dedicated at least two years each without pay in sharing the gospel message as world emissaries, a work they now continue indirectly through their singing.

The Choir has no butcher, baker, or candlestick maker, but it does have a farmer, a banker, and a typesetter. The largest occupational group is, predictably, housewife/homemaker, with sixty-seven in that category, followed by thirty-five schoolteachers, seventeen secretaries, eleven music teachers, ten accountants, nine sales representatives, and nine doctors or dentists. Also among their number are the executive director of the Utah Symphony, a university research director, a mail carrier, two barbers, a lawyer, and a wedding consultant—all uniting to make music.

Enrollment was reduced by attrition to 310 by early 1979, and Choir leaders intend to stabilize the Choir at a slightly larger number. A smaller Choir than in the past does not result in a significant reduction of vocal power, according to Dr. Ottley, and the smaller Choir is actually more manageable, as well as less expensive to maintain. Ottley's optimum Choir will have 320 voices—168 women and 152 men—with 42 singers on each of the four women's parts and 38 in each of the four men's sections (soprano, alto, tenor, and bass sections are each divided, making an eight-part choir).

The individual influence of these singers is widely felt throughout the communities from which they come. Four of every five conduct congregational singing, two out of five are organists, and more than ninety percent sing in local Church choirs. More than half are themselves choir directors. One-fifth of the Choir members are public-school music teachers, and one-fourth are private music teachers. At least sixty percent either have taken or are taking voice lessons, and one in five are individual performers, while a total of twenty-two members are composers and thirty-one are arrangers of music.

A concert trip is both an opportunity and an additional burden. Most of those who go on the extended tours of two weeks or more must use their annual vacations for the trip, arrange for substitutes, or take leave without pay from their jobs. But Choir tours serve an important function for them. So much of their effort is in broadcasts and recordings, separated from their millions of listeners, and on the concert tour, those live audiences provide the direct response on which musical performers feed. Also, the tours often provide travel opportunities which many Choir members might otherwise not have. Though the work is hard and the schedule demanding, they travel free, and experience the gratification of the joyful impact of their labors on those for whom they work so many hours without financial reward.

Chameleonlike, Choir members on tour alternate between being polished performers on the concert stage and gawking tourists off. The morning after a performance, reviews by the music critics are sought as eagerly as if each singer had made his or her debut. They are awe struck whenever an important conductor, music writer, guest soloist, or prominent politician tells them how good they really are.

This naïve joy which the singers feel as they contribute to a cause much larger than themselves, coupled with the genuine brotherhood they feel for each other, has virtually rid the Choir of any problems due to temperamental prima donnas. Even the members chosen as soloists greet each opportunity with honest humility, knowing that others could do the job equally well, and are confident that the entire Choir is pulling for them during their brief moment in the limelight. It is their combination of competence and humility, enthusiasm and modesty, which endears the Choir to other musicians.

There are occasions when the modesty and humility is richly deserved. A former Choir director reluctantly halted a disastrous start on a complicated and unorthodox arrangement the Choir was sight-reading for the first time. "No group of musicians in the world can rise to such inspiring heights," he said, "—or founder so magnificently on an unfamiliar musical score!"

13

Sing unto the Nations

A FOREST OF MICROPHONES rises above the symphony orchestra and Choir, their cables strung across the platform and disappearing out of sight through a doorway. Singers and instrumentalists are in shirt-sleeves, dressed for comfort instead of appearance; the Tabernacle has been cleared of all spectators. At the other end of the cables, in a basement room used as a recording studio, sit two 32-mm. magnetic tape recorders, an elaborate mixing console, and four loud-speakers. Behind them are the producer and two engineers from Columbia Records. Upstairs, the conductor wields a baton over the assembled forces, but there is no doubt that the disembodied voice which reaches them through the under-seat speakers is in command, the voice of the producer saying, "Very good, but one more time, please."

It is an October night in 1978, and Columbia Records is making a new album, scheduled for release a year later, before the Christmas buying season. It will feature American baritone Sherrill Milnes, the Salt Lake Mormon Tabernacle Choir, and the Columbia Symphony Orchestra, all under the direction of Dr. Jerold Ottley.

It is a routine the Tabernacle Choir has repeated many times in its long history, often with accompaniment by such notable ensembles as the Philadelphia Orchestra, the New York Philharmonic, and the Royal Philharmonic, occasionally with featured soloists and always with a mixture of excitement and frustration.

Recordings are probably the least satisfying and rewarding of all the Choir's activities. Choir members invariably come away gratified from their three General Conference sessions every six months. There is appropriate praise from the pulpit and an electric sense of communion with the audience from every corner of the world who take great pride in the Choir's reputation in their own lands.

The broadcasts—fifty-two of them every year—are the Choir's "bread-and-butter" fare. The rewards are simple: rapt attention followed by warm applause from an appreciative audience in the Tabernacle and a vaguely personal, if unseen, host of listeners and viewers who keep up a sporadic correspondence with the Choir.

For most members, concert tours are the "frosting on the cake," combining travel, recreation, companionship, and enthusiastic response from almost every performance; and there are reviews in the morning papers. But tours are immensely expensive, and can never produce enough income to cover costs.

By contrast, there is little immediate satisfaction from a recording session. It is grueling, time-consuming, repetitive work, with only the producer's "Bravo!" over the loudspeakers to let them know they have performed adequately. When Choir members finally receive the album they worked so hard to produce, months will have passed; it will almost sound like some other choir, from another place, coming over the home stereo system. There will be a few reviews in recording magazines and newspaper columns, and only occasional letters from record buyers.

Most exasperating of all is the recognition that learning and recording the new music is often a dead end and always done on "overtime." Few of the pieces will be repeated for General Conference, the broadcasts, or the concert hall. Similarly, while some members, including Jerold Ottley, welcome the diversion and challenge represented by the excellent, often unorthodox, arrangements performed only for recordings, others believe the Choir's musical standards are compromised whenever the music is not sacred or classical.

However, there is one area in which the recordings are extremely satisfying. The royalties from the commercial sales of popular and classical records and tapes ultimately make possible the new serious music and new costumes used in the broadcasts and concerts, and without that income, the concert tours would be virtually impossible to finance.

The album the Choir is currently recording with Sherrill Milnes will include inspirational and optimistic tunes from Broadway shows and motion pictures, numbers like "Look to the Rainbow," "Oklahoma!" and "On a Clear Day You Can See Forever." There are ten pieces in all, the Choir's standard disc format due to copyright regulations and other business considerations.

The album's musical arranger is Arthur Harris, who has arranged several recent Choir recordings and also conducted on two albums where the Choir and orchestra were separately recorded. Harris's arrangements usually fit the Choir's range and musical abilities very well.

The fifty-five-piece "Columbia Symphony" (actually, members of the Utah Symphony) is performing the orchestral parts. They are seated on a special platform which juts out from the rostrum and covers the first several rows of seats in the auditorium.

The Choir has been rehearsing the Harris arrangements for about four weeks by extending the Thursday and Sunday rehearsals, using two singers from the Choir, Don Becker and Robert van Wagenen, as stand-ins on the baritone solos.

During the final rehearsal, Ottley commented, "I would just like to say how I feel almost schizophrenic at this time. Here I am ready to conduct a recording session with an orchestra which has never before seen the music and playing from parts which have never been played from, and with a consummate musician [Milnes] standing at my side. If I seem a little nervous I think that you can all understand why."

Sixteen microphone channels will be used, one for the soloist, four for the Choir, and the rest for sections of the orchestra. These sixteen channels will be mixed down into four tracks and recorded. CBS uses two simultaneously running tape machines as insurance against one possibly malfunctioning.

The challenge of recording in the Tabernacle is learning to cope with the resonance which is such an integral part of the building's acoustics. A producer does not want the basic sound of the Choir to get lost in the tonal wash and reverberation of the building, particularly in "pop" material. In religious compositions, more reverberation suggests the churches for which such music was composed. "The Tabernacle is something of a problem because of the acoustics," says Columbia producer Tom Frost, "but it's not insurmountable. I've gotten used to working there. I continue to be shocked the first time I hear something. But we somehow solve it and it's comfortable to work in."

The recording session begins, as do all Choir activities, with a prayer. Milnes, who came in a few minutes earlier to say hello to the recording staff, is off in a basement practice room, warming up.

Then the producer goes up to the auditorium. "I just want to say hello." "Hello!" answers the Choir and Frost's face lights up. "I'm happy to be back in Salt Lake City. I look forward to working with you once again."

Next comes the testing of the recording levels. He asks each instrumental section, and then sections of the Choir, to play or sing a few notes. The engineers move some of the instrumentalists around and bring the mikes closer into the chorus. A few minutes and the sessions are ready to go. The producer communicates with the conductor privately through a telephone unit and uses closed-circuit television to watch the conductor and soloist.

" 'On a Clear Day' . . . take one." The session starts without the soloist, to give the chorus and orchestra a good warm-up and to concentrate on the basic sound. Frost lets the first take run through to the end of the piece. There are problems: a wrong entrance or two, a lack of synchronization between chorus and orchestra, a general feeling of tentativeness. Par for a first take.

A recording is different, psychologically and technically, from a live performance. With no audience, the performers are less emotionally involved. A recording must be more note-perfect than a live performance. Details which would scarcely be noticed live become glaring errors when heard, repeated dozens of times, on a record. However, a producer must create an atmosphere in which the performers are musically inspired.

Frost generally likes to do long takes. He tries to run through the entire piece, particularly those in relatively short arrangements. With a flowing, ongoing sound, he can edit without altering the basic feel of a performance.

173

Producer and conductor confer over the phone on matters of balance and tempo. "Take two." The women do not come in together with the orchestra. Frost stops immediately, and goes "back to the top." In his cool professionalism, there is no hint of criticism; simply, "Let's take that again," and an announcement for "take three." Ottley asks for a few moments of untaped rehearsal time. On the third take, the entry is perfect and the performance goes on, once again to the conclusion of the piece.

There are a few retakes of problem sections. One of Frost's techniques is to avoid numbering every start consecutively, since performers' spirits can sag as the number grows larger. He calls sections being recorded to fix a specific spot "inserts." "Take nine, insert four." The take numbers are called out over the loudspeaker system so that they are recorded on the tape; this identifies the segments for editing months later, with an annotated list of takes provided for each piece.

Usually, producers schedule three three-hour sessions for an album of ten selections. This recording will be done in two sessions of three and a half hours each. "The Choir is very well trained, and Jerry has a very efficient way with them," explains the producer. Their dedication and professionalism makes it possible to complete a recording of high quality in less time than it takes many professional ensembles.

For the next song of the album, the soloist joins the assembled performers, bringing along his scores and a Thermos of juice. He stands facing the Choir and conductor, his back to the empty hall. (Milnes expressed the wish that his mother, whom he remembers as a faithful listener of the Choir's broadcasts, could have lived to hear him perform with them.)

Like the Choir, Sherrill Milnes is identified with classical, rather than popular, music. But he approaches popular music with as much care as the operatic repertoire and a recording session with the same craftsmanship as a live performance. As an operatic star, he knows how much a gesture or facial expression can influence what an audience thinks it is hearing. On a record this same intensity must be conveyed purely through sound.

"Bravo!" says the voice in the loudspeakers, indicating that the producer has all the material he needs to edit a perfect composite version. When the voice occasionally says "Bravissimo!" the performers are understandably pleased with themselves. As one singer observed, "It is the only payment we get." A "bravo" has entered into the Choir's vocabulary. When members feel they have done a particularly good job of singing a piece at the sessions, one will often turn to a neighbor and say, "Now, *that* was a 'bravo!' "

The Choir members enjoy hearty snacks of cheese and juice during intermissions, and pass the time between takes with talk and jokes. But mostly they work, concentrating, performing with lots of energy. Every wasted minute, multiplied by 300 members, is a waste of five man-hours.

The sessions over, Ottley thanks the Choir and orchestra, Milnes says goodbye, and Frost and his engineers begin to pack. One engineer asks where he can get any of the older recordings made by J. Spencer Cornwall in the early 1950s.

Jerold Ottley leading the choir during a recording session.

He wants to hear if the old recordings had something that today's records lack. His professional work with the Choir has become a matter of some devotion.

The sessions have ended late Wednesday evening. The next night, the Choir has to be back in their seats at 7:30 for the rehearsal of next Sunday's broadcast. Soloist, conductor, and producer listen to a few final playbacks, go to dinner together, and then shake hands before going their separate ways. In a few months the four-channel master tapes will be mixed down to two-track form, from which Frost, after Ottley's approval, will edit the final composite for release.

The new album resulted from the interchange of ideas between Milnes, Columbia's Frost, and Evans and Ottley of the Choir. An earlier Choir album, *Climb Every Mountain,* had sold impressively (180,000 copies since its release ten years ago). Its theme was inspirational without being religious, drawing songs from Broadway shows. A sequel was proposed, and the Choir showed interest.

Meanwhile, Sherrill Milnes had been talking with Columbia about doing a selection of early American songs. Frost suggested the joint effort to Oakley Evans and Jerold Ottley. They were enthusiastic, and so was Milnes. Together, they decided on the songs, and recognized that an orchestral accompaniment was required.

A bicentennial album, *Yankee Doodle Dandies,* was recorded by the Choir in collaboration with Robert Merrill, and accompanied by Utah Symphony musicians under the name of the Columbia Symphony Orchestra. The combination, repeated on the album with Milnes, was a logical solution to a problem Columbia had wrestled with in different ways.

Collaboration with the Philadelphia Orchestra, the New York Philharmonic, or some other major symphony means moving either Choir or orchestra, and makes sense only when other concert tour commitments have already covered transportation expenses. On two albums, including *Climb Every Mountain,* the Choir parts were recorded first in the Tabernacle—without accompaniment—and the orchestra was separately rehearsed and recorded to synchronize with the singers. While eliminating travel, this process can wind up being more expensive; making the orchestra match perfectly with the prerecorded Choir is time-consuming and costly. Also, a record made this way sounds stiff; the rhythms are wooden and inflexible, and there is no aesthetic bond between the two groups of musicians.

Hence the decision to use musicians close to the Choir's home. The Utah Symphony has performed under its conductor, Maurice Abravanel, in the Tabernacle for a quarter of a century, and has recorded there regularly for Vanguard and EMI (Angel). In recent years, the Choir and the Utah Symphony have joined forces in concert, performing commissioned bicentennial works by Mormon composer Crawford Gates, and have also recorded another major Mormon work, *Book of Mormon Oratorio,* by Leroy Robertson, under Maestro Abravanel.

Thomas Frost, the man who brought the groups together, is director of artists and repertoire for Columbia Records. He has produced all the Choir's records since the mid-sixties, and the Choir is one of the few groups to which he still devotes his talents as a producer. He says simply, "I enjoy working with the

Tabernacle Choir. Their sound is very smooth and rich, each section has a very good blend; you seldom hear voices sticking out. It has a rich, mellow sound, a beautiful sound. Making albums with the Choir is fun." For both Columbia Records and the Choir, it has also been profitable.

If ever there was a musical marriage "made in Heaven" it came in the union of the Tabernacle Choir and the Philadelphia Orchestra. They collaborated on two albums which made "gold" by amassing one million dollars in sales. A third record, a collaboration with the New York Philharmonic and Leonard Bernstein, is also a "gold" record. One of the prized displays in the Choir president's office is a framed parchment of appreciation signed by Eugene Ormandy and each member of the Philadelphia Orchestra.

Association with the Philadelphia Orchestra dates back to May 5, 1936, when Leopold Stokowski and the orchestra visited Salt Lake City to perform in the Tabernacle. Stokowski invited the Choir to perform the "Hallelujah Chorus" with the orchestra as the finale, which received a tumultuous ovation. Stokowski turned to the audience and asked: "Wasn't that thrilling?"

The orchestra returned the next year with its new music director, Eugene Ormandy, and collaborated this time with the Choir in excerpts from Wagner's *Die Meistersinger.* Ormandy's comment: "I wish we had such a chorus in Philadelphia." His wish was answered twenty-one years later during the Choir's concert tour of 1958, which included three performances and a recording of *Messiah* with the orchestra in Philadelphia.

But the musical courtship during that tour had a shaky beginning. The Choir's train was late and the singers missed part of the rehearsal; the Maestro was obviously upset. He introduced the orchestra to the Choir and began to work on the first chorus of *Messiah,* "And the Glory of the Lord." The Choir was nervous and wanted to make amends. They did. "We hit it," remembers one Choir member. "Oh, man, did we hit it!" Ormandy beamed to his orchestra, and said: "I told you, you would like them." The orchestra answered with bravos.

The first performance was a matinee, usually attended by an older, less demonstrative audience. The concert was greeted with a standing ovation, the first Ormandy ever recalled at a matinee. The performances on two successive nights were equally well received, and recordings were made the following day. Actually, only half the Choir members were present for the recording session, since there was not adequate space in the hotel ballroom in which the recordings were made, and part of the Choir was in New York City for an appearance on the Ed Sullivan television show.

The "gold" *Messiah* album was recorded at Ormandy's request. Even though it would compete with another Columbia recording of the same work by the New York Philharmonic, Goddard Lieberson, Columbia's top man, said, "I like competition," and an independent backer guaranteed a large part of the costs.

The Choir's recording relationship with the Philadelphia Orchestra continued over the next twelve years. They produced an exceptional series of records, ranging from their finest recording of a major oratorio, the Brahms *Requiem,* to several delightful Christmas albums. The word that keeps being repeated in discussions with Ormandy about the Choir is *blend*. He remarks that there are no weak sections in the Choir and, conversely, no one section ever stands out from the others. "And they listen," he adds. "They do what I ask them to. They are a great choir like my orchestra is a great orchestra. With all respect to the wonderful choirs on the East Coast, the Mormon Tabernacle Choir is the greatest choir in the world."

Ormandy is respected and beloved by the Choir as much as he evidently respects the Choir itself. It was an ideal marriage, Ormandy once said, not between two great musical organizations, but between one great combined ensemble and a conductor. But when the Philadelphia Orchestra switched to a competing record label, further joint recordings were effectively annulled, although combined concerts are still a possibility.

Recording exclusively for Columbia since 1949, the Choir has released more than forty-five long-playing albums. When you include those albums on which the Choir appears only on one cut, or track, the number on which their music appears climbs to ninety. Most of them, being classical releases, are still available. Several have sold more than 100,000 copies, including at least three Christmas albums.

But the United States isn't the only country where the Choir's records are popular. Subsidiary Columbia companies in many parts of the world are independently producing recordings by the Tabernacle Choir, choosing titles, designs, and selections different from those available in the U.S.A., and boosting both the Choir's fame and the royalties.

The Choir, however, now faces a dilemma. It has always been an organization identified with classical music. In fact, Jerry Ottley would like to see the Choir increasingly respected in choral music circles and making more classical recordings. One of his recent albums, *A Jubilant Song*, is a selection of twentieth-century American choral pieces, featuring compositions by Howard Hanson, Randall Thompson, and other established American figures. Each is a first recording, and, since Ottley feels it is the Choir's duty to encourage and perform music by Mormon and western musicians, several are by Utah composers. It is, therefore, the most "serious" recording of recent years, but it will never become a gold record. With the Choir dependent on royalties as its major income, the popular forms of music which bring in the greatest revenue must continue as a major part of the Choir's recording activity. Hopefully, though, a balance can be reached in which the popular albums will provide revenues to subsidize the classical projects.

14

Good Tidings

Before the H-bomb, before the atomic age, before World War II, before "the long presidency," before Hitler, before the Japanese seized Manchuria, before the Great Depression, and even before the Wall Street crash, long, long ago on July 15, 1929, a great 375-voice choir began broadcasting coast-to-coast from the Salt Lake City Tabernacle. Every Sunday morning in the intervening years, winter and summer, war or peace, rain or shine, it has broadcast its half-hour of hymns old and new, of Bach and Handel and of all the sweet and stately and spine-tingling sounds from the whole library of Christendom's sacred music. Behind the 375 voices swells an organ of 10,000 pipes.

These words, in a *Life* magazine editorial of July 26, 1954, marked the first twenty-five years of the Choir's broadcasts. Another quarter-century has passed since, and the Choir's audience is even larger, and with the addition of television, more personal. Behind this series of more than 2,600 programs is a weekly ritual which makes the thirty-minute program possible.

The cycle for the next week's broadcast of "Music and the Spoken Word" begins immediately after the previous program ends. Choir, conductor, and organists can listen on Sunday evenings to a KSL rebroadcast of that morning's program. The music staff also reviews a tape recording. On Tuesday, the music staff meets with the television technicians to watch a videotape recording and plan the next show. On Thursday night the Choir rehearses, primarily focusing on the Sunday broadcast music. Then, on Sunday morning, comes the dress rehearsal, camera run-through, and, finally, the broadcast/television program itself.

The Choir rehearses every Thursday evening from 7:30 to 9:30. Members enter the Tabernacle through the special Choir entrance. From the rows and rows of numbered slots, members pick up their music folders. If a slot is empty, the member is marked "present"—a roll-taking system established by J. Spencer Cornwall. Absences are not taken lightly; morale and musical values both suffer when people are not consistent. If Choir members are absent more than twenty percent of the time, they are on probation; if attendance does not improve, they are invited to resign. Serious illness is a valid excuse, and singers may apply for a justified leave of absence.

At 7:25, the singers take their assigned seats: sopranos, altos, tenors, basses —from the conductor's left to his right. The seating area is a semicircular amphitheater, sharply rising, with the conductor's podium as the focal point. Sightlines are excellent; because of the steep pitch of the seats, no one feels too far from the conductor. For years, individual seats were claimed on the basis of seniority. However, Ottley now places people by their vocal characteristics or, for concert tours, by their height.

Audiences are always present for rehearsals as well as the broadcasts, making both events something of a concert. Spectators are admitted at 8:00 P.M. after announcements and business have been presented by President Oakley S. Evans, who often reads letters from radio listeners or Tabernacle broadcast guests. It is the reward for which the singers do their work. The letters are also a reminder of their responsibilities to the Church and to their audience.

Some typical excerpts from radio listeners:

Thank you—thank you—again and again! Every Sunday
the broadcast of the Choir and the Spoken Word is a
very special time for my brief early worship.

—Crofton, Maryland
July 16, 1978

Just a short letter to let you know how much I enjoy
your Sunday broadcasts over WCCO-Radio, Minneapolis.
I am a choir director myself so the program is always of
special interest since I love music!

—Brooten, Minneapolis
July 16, 1978

Being old and unable to attend local services, I derive
a great deal of comfort and inspiration from your
service. . . .

—Pacific Palisades, California
March 30, 1977

Being a soloist and teacher I feel I am qualified to say
that the quality of your program, which has been so
consistent through the years, far exceeds any other being
aired today.

—Ocean City, New Jersey
January, 1976

And from television viewers:

I was deeply impressed by the sincerity and
wholesomeness portrayed by both men and women who
contribute their talents and efforts to the Mormon
Tabernacle Choir.

Rochester, New York
August 21, 1977

It has been my intention before now to write to you and
to compliment you on the most excellent production of
your TV program which we here listen to with very great
enthusiasm.
The singing of the Choir, the organ music and the
"Spoken Word" are certainly a great tonic to us in these
so very troublesome times. The inspiration of it all gives
us a great faith in the future and we can but hope that
your activities may last for a very long time.

—Johannesburg, South Africa
December 28, 1976

Your program exudes nothing but beauty, and *never* fails
to bring tears to my eyes.

—Topanga, California
February 22, 1976

President Evans concludes these preliminaries by requesting a member to
pray. The member invokes the Lord's blessings for the Choir's activities, for
someone who is sick that day, for the officers of the Church and the Choir.

With the public now admitted, the rehearsal begins, and the music staff takes
over. Jerry Ottley is making a concerted effort to develop the singers' vocal
capabilities. The Choir had been noted for a particular sound, rich but rather
monochromatic; it was an excellent vocal format for certain parts of the repertoire, less suitable for others. Ottley seeks a more flexible and varied aural spec-
trum, a Choir that utilizes a broad palette of styles and textures.

The rehearsal often starts with warm-up exercises designed to nurture the
Choir's growing repertoire of vocal techniques. Next, he may ask the Choir to
sing a given pattern in different styles and rhythmic inflections, sung first with a
"Brahms sound," then a "Mozart" or a "French" sound. (The Sunday morning
warm-ups are even more important; the vocal cords are usually not yet limber at
7:45 A.M.)

As the rehearsal proceeds, visitors become aware of the Tabernacle's
unusual acoustics. Its roof seems completely unsupported; there is a sense of

vastness. Since it was built as an orator's hall, a speaker at the pulpit can be heard throughout the building. In a popular demonstration, visitors sit at one end of the building while a guide drops a small nail onto a wooden block at the other; it is clearly heard, as is a whisper. The Choir singers themselves, however, have difficulty hearing other sections. Similarly, the balance of sound changes as listeners move to different parts of the hall. The curved ceiling behind the Choir and organ serves as a resonant shell and gives the Choir a quality never duplicated in other halls. Many are convinced the Choir's sound is better elsewhere, while others believe the hall's ambience and echoes effectively hide a multitude of vocal sins.

Broadcast technicians attend every rehearsal, to familiarize themselves with the music to be performed on the weekend and to record and time a run-through of each number for Ottley, enabling him to hear how the music will sound on the air. The audience is reminded to be silent during taping by a wonderful old blue neon sign, like one from a 1940 ice cream parlor, which reads, BROADCASTING.

A copy of the tape goes to the television director, who listens to the music and begins to visualize how best to represent the performance on the video screen; by Sunday morning the exact moment of every transition, cut, and zoom will be neatly marked on the score.

Dr. Ottley's rehearsal technique is to treat the Choir as if they were professional musicians, talking through problems as he runs through the piece. A microphone is hung about his neck and is plugged into the underseat speakers, enabling him to give verbal instructions without interrupting the music. Singers keep pencils ready and mark the instructions on their parts.

Typically, a selection will be previewed and sight-read briefly one week, reviewed in detail a week later, and then polished on the third week for broadcast the following Sunday morning. Inasmuch as a typical broadcast includes six musical selections, some twenty different pieces are included in each rehearsal. Rehearsal time for recordings must also be squeezed in; occasionally Tuesday rehearsals are added, and there is usually a rehearsal following the Sunday broadcasts.

The Thursday night rehearsal is basically two solid hours of work, with a stretch (but no intermission) after the first hour. The Choir's concentration is phenomenal; union musicians would never accept their schedule.

Television is a more complex and demanding medium than radio, and much of the Sunday morning rehearsal is occupied by the television crew. Even before the first Choir members arrive at the Tabernacle, the television technicians are already reviewing their scripts and equipment and conferring with the Choir director for the morning's broadcast. Both conductors are there (in the event of an emergency, the other is ready), as are organists Robert Cundick and John Longhurst, together with Udell Poulsen and President Oakley Evans. They gather in the organists' small office and kneel together in prayer, asking the blessing of the Lord as they perform service in His name. Then another hectic Sunday morning schedule begins.

When the Biglers, the Wilsons, and the other singers arrive at the Tabernacle, it will still be two hours before the program goes on the air, at 9:30 A.M. Mountain Standard Time. Arriving Choir members don their uniform of the day —rust jackets and gold shirts for the men and matching copper blouses and black skirts for the women.

Meanwhile, a preproduction meeting of the television staff is held between cameramen, the lighting technician, time controller, and director Mike Mischler. Additional crew and equipment are in a large semitrailer parked outside. Working from detailed scripts, they first talk the program through, then begin camera rehearsals, under the watchful eye of producer Mike McLean.

Three television cameras are in place, one at the back of the hall, another mounted on a dolly on a platform in front of the Choir, the third among the choir seats. Beneath the gallery at the conductor's left are the audio and video control booths; behind their glass windows are two teams of technicians. The audio director, Ray Loveless, has placed four microphones in the Choir, four for the organ, and has suspended a stereo microphone from the ceiling. Mixing and balancing, he controls the sound of Choir, organ, and hall reverberations. The audio program is fed to the CBS network lines, to the tape recorders, and to the television control room.

Donald Ripplinger is in the control booth at 9:25 A.M.

Awaiting the down-beat which will begin the broadcast is senior Tabernacle organist Dr. Robert Cundick. Not only will he provide the Choir's accompaniment, but he also will perform a three-to-five minute organ solo. The Tabernacle audience is not aware that the performance has been prerecorded for radio and television to permit greater audio, camera, and lighting flexibility, making it perhaps the most visually interesting part of the program. For the Tabernacle audience, he repeats the selection while maintaining the timing by listening to a small speaker which plays back his own recorded performance.

Shortly before 9:30, commentator J. Spencer Kinard greets the audience and tells them about the broadcast they are about to see. Through close cooperation and planning, musical text and the "Spoken Word" are usually linked to a common theme, and Spencer Kinard's script will start or end with a key phrase from the music which precedes or follows his weekly sermonette. The moments tick by and, a few seconds short of 9:30, he takes his place before camera one, ready to open the show.

The Choir is seated, ready to sing. At a complicated electrical panel, the lighting technician runs a final check. At his whim, the Tabernacle becomes a mammoth television studio, its white plaster ceiling suddenly a royal blue. Ned Huntsman has been at the Tabernacle for more than seventeen years. When he first began working on the television show, the Tabernacle's lighting equipment was rudimentary. He installed a computerized system eight years ago, giving the show a professional gloss. Suspended from the ceiling of the Tabernacle are six light battens ranging from fifteen to thirty feet long. Installed in these strips are two dozen 5,000-watt lights and numerous 1,000-watters. Even the Tabernacle chandeliers contain four separate circuits which can light the auditorium but not the ceiling or vice versa.

The prerecorded material is ready to roll, the preset lights are ready to go —at the push of a button. Inside the broadcast booth it is like the moment before a race: everyone is straining ahead, his attention aimed straight front. Mike counts: "Five, four, three, two, one, we're on the air."

"Gently Raise the Sacred Strain," a hymn by Thomas Griggs, former assistant conductor of the Choir, begins each broadcast. The balance of the music is chosen by the conductor or the assistant conductor, Don Ripplinger, who is responsible for one broadcast a month. Each begins to work on the program at least two months in advance, and both are guided by similar considerations.

The Choir provides a generalized program of inspirational music which can apply to most faiths. The music is often from Protestant composers, occasionally from Roman Catholic or Jewish composers. Secular pieces, including folk songs, are frequently scheduled. Every broadcast includes a short familiar hymn which can be expanded or shortened by adding or deleting a verse, as signaled inconspicuously by the conductor, even after the broadcast is under way. This and the opening and closing themes are the only constants in the musical formula.

A conductor must be an efficiency expert when he programs the broadcast. The Choir works on a pressure-cooker schedule, preparing six or seven new pieces a week in addition to music for tours and recordings or General Conferences. Extremely difficult pieces are hard to justify in terms of the time they require. Often, Ottley programs a piece which half of the Choir can sing from memory. Programming an "old favorite" not only allows the conductor more rehearsal time for other works, it also is a big lift to the Choir, for they can just sing a song and enjoy it without having to dig quite so hard.

Under a succession of five conductors since the broadcasts began, the Choir has continued to have favorite music. Some of it is seasonal and turns up almost every year: Thanksgiving, Easter, Christmas, and the annual July observance which commemorates the arrival of their pioneer forefathers in 1847. The titles that show up most frequently are the cherished and familiar hymns, some of them being used two and three times during a given year.

Jerry Ottley observes, "A lot of our listeners have taken a proprietary interest in the Choir to the extent that they let us know very strongly what they like and what they don't like." The Choir receives hundreds of letters a week from its listeners, providing them with a good barometer of public reaction. Unfortunately, reactions aren't always positive. The core of the Choir's audience, which is in the over-thirty age group, often indicate that they find the music written in a more contemporary idiom "unsettling." Yet, Ottley is committed to the music of this century, and he is willing to raise a few hackles.

"Music and the Spoken Word" has no sponsorship. Radio and television stations carry the program as a public service, broadcasting nationwide over the CBS-Radio network. Within the United States approximately 140 stations carry "Music and the Spoken Word" live and another 430 release it from tape record-

Ray Loveless, audio engineer, monitoring a broadcast

ings at other times. The television show is broadcast live in the Salt Lake City area on its parent station and is shown by videotape on 40 other stations. Fourteen cable systems also feed the program to their subscribers. Tape recordings of the radio program are also heard on stations in Great Britain, Canada, Italy, New Zealand, Samoa, the West Indies, the Philippines, and the Netherlands Antilles, and on the United States Armed Forces Network overseas.

"As the Dew from Heaven Distilling" by Joseph Daynes, the first Tabernacle organist, is played on the organ to close the program. It is ten o'clock, and the broadcast is over. The Choir hands back the finished music, goes backstage for a quick break, and gets ready for the short rehearsal which immediately follows the broadcast. Thoughts are already turning to Sunday dinner, to families, perhaps to an afternoon ward choir rehearsal and the afternoon or evening worship service.

The Biglers and the Wilsons, the Ottleys and the Ripplingers have been in the Tabernacle for nearly four hours this Sunday morning. Soon they will doff their choir costumes, and their choir duties, for today. Four days later, however, the cycle will start again, as they once again return to the Tabernacle.

It is a time of milestones for these Mormon music makers. Their first network radio broadcast was 50 years ago; their first recordings were 70 years back. It is 112 years since they moved into the Tabernacle, and 132 years since they first performed in the pioneer settlement.

The Salt Lake Mormon Tabernacle Choir is the primary musical organization of The Church of Jesus Christ of Latter-day Saints. It is, like its parent Church, an organization of strong commitment and intense emotional ties. And like its parent Church, it is growing and active, its membership alive with their love of their religion and their fellow men. The Choir will inevitably change in the future. It will be beset by pressures of commercialism and changing fashion. It is apparent, however, that the Choir will stand as a beacon for those who believe in the strength of music and of faith to help the world grow into what it should become.

Members
–Past and Present–
of The Mormon Tabernacle Choir

Abbott, Charles
Abbott, John
Abegg, Louise. *See* Clarke, Louise Abegg
Adair, Mrs.
Adams, Ann Rogerson, Mrs.
Adams, Beth W.
Adams, Clara
Adams, Don L.
Adams, E. Harris
Adams, Homer E.
Adams, Joseph
Adams, Lucy
Adams, P., Miss
Adams, Selia
Adamson, Corinne, Mrs.
Adamson, Edith, Miss
Adamson, Helen
Adamson, John C. (Jack)
Adkins, Sherry Pratt
Aird, Eva, Mrs.
Aird, Jack A.
Airmet, Kathy R., Mrs.
Akert, John
Alba, Edna, Miss
Albecht, May
Albisten, Thomas
Albrechtsen, Christine
Alder, Florence H.
Alder, Mae C.
Aldous, H. M.
Aldous, Janet C., Mrs.
Aldrich, Melba
Allen, Adele
Allen, Arintha
Allen, Dorothy
Allen, Elaine
Allen, Julia
Allen, Lynn L.
Allen, Mary E.
Allen, Patricia
Allen, William F.
Alley, Stephen L.
Allgaier, H. J.
Allison, Bessie Dean
Allred, C. Evan
Allred, Dorothy
Allred, G. Hugh
Allred, Garth W.
Allred, Karen Leishman, Mrs.
Allred, Viola Blunck, Mrs.
Allsop, Donna
Almond, Max E.
Almond, Reese A.
Almstead, Lydia
Alsop, Donna
Alviston, T. H.

Ames, Catherine
Ames, George
Amott, Robert D.
Amundsen, Eugene
Anastasiou, Yvonne
Anderegg, Henry Edward
Anderegg, Montess M., Mrs.
Andersen, Pearl
Andersen, Vinnie
Anderson, Agnes, Mrs.
Anderson, Alex P.
Anderson, Alice Bickerstaff
Anderson, Andrea. *See* Whitney, Andrea Anderson
Anderson, Anna, Mrs.
Anderson, Christine
Anderson, Darrell L.
Anderson, David P.
Anderson, Doyle R.
Anderson, Elaine. *See* Card, Elaine Anderson
Anderson, Elizabeth G.
Anderson, Elna Jean, Miss
Anderson, Eunice Whipple, Mrs.
Anderson, Frank Charles
Anderson, Fred Y.
Anderson, Howard T.
Anderson, Ivy
Anderson, James S.
Anderson, Joan Ellen. *See* Fox, Joan Ellen Anderson
Anderson, Joseph M.
Anderson, Joyce H.
Anderson, Lawrence Dick
Anderson, Linda. *See* Zeeman, Linda Anderson
Anderson, Marc W.
Anderson, Mary L.
Anderson, Melba
Anderson, Nephi
Anderson, Phil
Anderson, R. Udell
Anderson, Richard
Anderson, Richmond
Anderson, Robert L.
Anderson, S. W.
Anderson, ShaRee B., Mrs.
Anderson, Sheldon
Anderson, Ted L.
Anderton, Lila Harvetin, Mrs.
Anderton, Norma Christensen, Mrs.
Andreasen, Una, Mrs.
Andrews, John W.
Andrews, Tennie
Andrus, Ilene
Andrus, Roman R.

Angel, Arthur
Angel, Truman O.
Angell, Alice
Angell, Stella
Angerbauer, Betty
Armistead, Arreva
Armitage, Nellie
Armstrong (Librarian)
Armstrong, Mary
Arnold, Vilate Smith, Mrs.
Around, A. L.
Ash, Thomas
Ashton, J. W.
Ashton, Louise Keddington, Mrs.
Ashton, Mark
Ashton, Norma
Ashton, Patricia S. *See* Grant, Patricia S.
Ashworth, Eladia
Ashworth, Eliza
Ashworth, Thomas
Aspinal, Rebecca
Aste, Margaret
Astin, J. N.
Astin, Merle. *See* Schreiner, Merle Astin
Astin, Patyra
Astle, Vivyenne
Athay, Donald R.
Atkinson, Bernard F.
Attridge, Earl Donald
Aubrey, William
Aupperle, Robert
Austin, Gordon P.
Austin, Kathryn. *See* Visher, Kathryn Austin
Aveson, R. F.

Babb, Patricia Jean. *See* Christenson, Patricia Babb
Backman, Mary Jean
Backman, G. H.
Bacon, Esther
Baddley, Maria
Baddley, Mary Lynn Pearce, Mrs.
Badger, Doris Martin, Mrs.
Bagley, A. Marie
Bagley, Estrid Fors, Mrs.
Bailey, Anna Fugal, Mrs.
Bailey, Esther
Bailey, J. W.
Bailey, Loile J.
Bailey, Rachel Whittaker
Bair, Laura C. G., Mrs.
Baker, Carlyle
Baker, Claire Moss, Mrs.
Baker, John W.

Baker, Moneta S., Mrs.
Ball, Edith. *See* Smith, Edith Ball
Ball, Lucille
Ballard, Seth
Balmforth, Charles
Bannatine, Jamesina. *See* Stoneman, Jamesina Bannatine
Barber, Cora
Barber, Fern
Barber, H. D.
Barber, H. E.
Bardsley, Stephen J.
Barker, Allan H.
Barker, Joanne, Mrs.
Barker, Laurel. *See* Ruhlfing, Laurel Barker
Barker, Meredith, Miss
Barker, O., Miss
Barlow, J. M.
Barlow, Jane
Barlow, June. *See* Burton, June Barlow
Barlow, Lillie
Barlow, Thelma
Barnes, Richard Lloyd
Barney, Rachael. *See* Read, Rachael Barney
Barney, Richard
Barraclough, Clyde
Barraclough, Harold F.
Barrell, Alice
Barrell, C. H.
Barrell, Elihu
Barrell, H. Charles
Barrett, Ellen
Barrows, Fred
Barrus, Ralph M.
Bartholomew, Alice Falkner, Mrs.
Barton, Miss
Basinger, David L.
Bassett, E. K.
Bassett, Maggie
Bate, Almon
Bateman, Harold E.
Bateman, Mary F., Mrs.
Bates, Derold E.
Bates, Edward F.
Baugh, George T.
Bauman, Gwenneth
Baur, Judith. *See* Chartrand, Judith Baur
Bawles, G.
Baxter, Mary
Baxter, Phyllis
Bayles, Sandra J.
Bayliss, Emma
Beach, Lois Olson

Bean, Evan
Beasley, William
Beatie, N. Ross
Beatie, Sue Smith, Mrs.
Beck, Dorothy Ence, Mrs.
Becker, Donald L.
Becker, Peggy, Mrs.
Beckstead, Lee A.
Beckstead, Lee A., Mrs.
Beckstead, Maurine, Miss
Beckstrand, Arnold
Beers, Ronald
Beers, William L.
Beesley, Adelbert
Beesley, Diane Heder, Mrs.
Beesley, Ebenezer
Beesley, Ebenezer, Jr.
Beesley, Ella
Beesley, Evangaline T., Mrs.
Beesley, Fred
Beesley, Fred
Beesley, Garratt Thomas
Beesley, William J.
Beeston, Ruby
Beezley, Emily Cooper
Behling, James R.
Behnke, J. Ray
Behunin, George Frank
Behunin, Joan Pitts, Mrs.
Behunin, Lynda
Behunin, Ruby
Beisinger, Jean
Belgique, Daniel
Bell, H. V.
Bellamy, Almina
Bellamy, Elizabeth
Bellamy, John R.
Belliston, Donna
Benard, Helen H. *See* Jensen,
    Helen Benard
Bennett, Beatrice
Bennett, Fred
Bennett, Lily
Bennett, Peter H.
Bennett, Susan. *See* Winters, Susan
    Bennett
Bennion, Mrs.
Bennion, Anne. *See* Jenson, Anne
    Bennion
Bennion, Carolyn Vance, Mrs.
Bennion, Donald D.
Bennion, Karla
Bennion, Merrill
Bennion, Wilma
Benson, Elda
Bentley, Joseph
Benzley, Janet
Berg, Mae V.
Bergenson, Andrew
Berghout, Cora
Berlin, Aleen
Berlin, Rose
Bernstrom, Harry
Berrett, Reed B.
Berry, Charles L.
Berry, Ellen
Best, Wendell
Bettridge, Doris
Bettridge, Eva May H., Mrs.
Bettridge, James
Bevis, F.
Beyer, Lucille Cardall, Mrs.
Bezooyen, Diena. *See* Van Bezoo-
    yen, Diena
Bickerstaff, Alice. *See* Anderson,
    Alice Bickerstaff
Bigler, Bonnie Rae Gardner, Mrs.
Bigler, David
Bigler, Gordon O.
Bigler, Hazel A., Mrs.
Bigler, L. Burt, Jr.
Bigler, Robert M.
Bingham, Keith J.
Bird, Alice R., Mrs.
Bird, C. W.
Bird, Charles R.
Bird, Clara M.
Bird, Gale
Bird, Hazel S., Mrs.
Bird, Heber G.

Bird, Lillian J.
Bird, Marian Bricker, Mrs.
Birkeland, Erline
Birrell, Arvilla
Bishop, Carolyn C.
Bishop, Klar
Bishop, Jay
Bishop, Lynn
Bishop, Marva
Bishop, Marvin
Bishop, Mariam D., Miss
Bishop, Zina. *See* Reed, Zina
    Bishop
Bitter, Charles
Bittner, Carol Jean
Bittner, Libbie
Bittner, May
Bixby, Hertha, Miss
Bixby, Lela
Bjorndal, Carol Jeanne. *See* Call,
    Carol Bjorndal
Black, Marie, Miss
Blackburn, A. L.
Blackhurst, Jonathan G. (Jon)
Blackhurst, Richard
Blackner, L. A.
Blair, Reva Brown
Blakemore, Erma Ridges
Blauer, Lorin R.
Bluck, Herbert
Bluhm, Louise
Boatright, Olive
Bocker, W. D.
Bockholt, Christine
Bodily, Keith
Boehme, Leah Loraine. *See* Bythe-
    way, Leah Loraine Boehme
Bolto, G. F.
Bolto, G. F., Mrs.
Boman, Clair Kent
Bond, Richard G.
Bonner, Nettie M.
Bons, Mariner A.
Bons, Peter
Booth, Elizabeth A.
Booth, Eva
Booth, H. E.
Booth, J. Kaye
Booth, J. K., Mrs.
Booth, L. H.
Booth, Lavern, Mrs.
Booth, Melba W.
Booth, Nan Chipman
Booth, Rebecca
Borgeson, J. V. T., Mrs.
Borgeson, Nettie
Borgeson, Rhoda
Borgquist, Dora V.
Bost, J. R.
Bourne, Alice. *See* Calder, Alice
    Bourne
Bourne, George E.
Bourne, Helen Whitney, Mrs.
Bowden, Robert
Bowen, Betsy Ila
Bowen, Garrick
Bowen, Lucile R.
Bowen, Lyle
Bowen, Wesley
Bowers, A.
Bowers, Carma Douglass, Mrs.
Bowers, Ioa Rowena
Bowers, Levi
Bowers, Mildred
Bowers, Orlando
Bowers, Ruth. *See* Robertson,
    Ruth B.
Bowler, J.
Bowman, Lorraine, Miss
Bowman, Nina N., Mrs.
Bowring, Bertie
Bowring, Maud
Bowring, W.
Boyce, E. D.
Boyd, Carl Stephen
Boyd, Kathleen Carter, Mrs.
Boyden, Walter E., Jr.
Boyer, Vivian
Braby, A. E.
Braby, Mamie

Bradford, Lillie
Bradford, Lisle
Bradford, Ray W.
Bradshaw, Dyca Ann Frisby
Bradshaw, Frank M.
Bradshaw, William
Bradson, Ethel
Brady, Jean
Brain, Carol Louise
Brain, E. J.
Braithwaite, Linda
Brandon, Tom
Branham, Arnold
Brewerton, L. P., Mrs.
Brewester, Maggie
Brewster, Beth Stevenson, Mrs.
Brewster, Bonnie
Brewster, Kyle Hayes
Bridges, Amy
Bright, John Wesley
Brimley, Barbara Hoppie, Mrs.
Brimley, Sharon. *See* Ockey,
    Sharon Brimley
Brimm, Martha Julia. *See* Tuck,
    Julia Brimm
Bringhurst, George
Brinton, Bonna Ashby
Brizee, Isabella. *See* Pardoe,
    Isabella Brizee
Broadbent, Janet Parry, Mrs.
Broadhead, Stephen R.
Brockbank, Gayle
Brockbank, H. D.
Brockbank, LaVon
Broderick, Adelia
Bromley, Haru Jane Speer
Brough, Eugene E.
Brough, Norma G.
Brough, Patricia
Brown, Calvin R.
Brown, Darrell Z.
Brown, Donald R.
Brown, Dorothy, Mrs.
Brown, Dorothy, Mrs.
Brown, Drusilla
Brown, Elsie
Brown, Emily
Brown, George C.
Brown, Gerty
Brown, LaPrele S.
Brown, May
Brown, Milo
Brown, Nathel
Brown, Nephi
Brown, Newel Kay
Brown, Reed
Brown, Richard
Brown, Ruby. *See* Gunderson,
    Ruby Brown
Brown, S. F., Miss
Brown, Shirley Johnson, Mrs.
Brown, Thelma. *See* Steiner,
    Thelma Brown
Brown, Thelma C.
Brown, William
Browning, Bessie, Mrs.
Brownson, A. V.
Bryggman, Britt-Marie. *See* Wras-
    pir, Britt Marie B.
Buckmiller, Richard G.
Budge, S. Elliott
Buehner, T.
Buie, Ismae, Miss
Bull, Hyrum J.
Bullock, Gene
Bult, Mary Louise
Burbidge, June
Burgess, Lurrine
Burgess, Roy
Burk, Caseel D.
Burkhart, Bruce E.
Burks, Ethel Louise. *See* Robinson,
    Ethel Burks
Burnett, Kenneth L.
Burnham, Barbara
Burnham, Perry H.
Burns, Cecil
Burns, Hattie
Burns, Linda
Burrell, Arthur L.

Burrell, E.
Burt, Sharon Faye Odell, Mrs.
Burton, Annette Jean
Burton, Dianne Marie Whitelock,
    Mrs.
Burton, Edith
Burton, Jacob
Burton, Jay P.
Burton, Julia
Burton, June Barlow, Mrs.
Burton, Mabel W., Mrs.
Burton, Robert S.
Burton, Shipley D.
Busby, Harley M.
Bush, Derylis Rowe Hill, Mrs.
Bush, Janeece. *See* Cook, Janeece
    Bush
Bush, W. Sterling
Bushman, Rex Bruce
Butler, F., Miss
Butler, Lloyd
Butler, Thomas
Butler, Thomas
Butterworth, Edward (or Edwin)
Buttle, Mary
Bybee, Barbara
Bytheway, Diane
Bytheway, Laraine Boehme
Bywater, Donna J., Mrs.
Bywater, Lizzie

Cahoon, Gomez B.
Caine, Mary Ellen
Calder, Alice Bourne, Mrs.
Calder, Maurice Hammond
Calder, Melvie
Calderwood, Myrna J.
Caldwell, Alfred
Caldwell, Ella Williams, Mrs.
Caldwell, Nettie
Caldwell, Shirley Ann
Calkins, L. A.
Call, Carol Jeanne Bjorndal, Mrs.
Call, Nina R.
Call, William G.
Callister, Genevieve Johns, Mrs.
Calton, Emma
Calton, George A.
Calton, J.
Calton, William
Cameron, D. E., Mrs.
Camomile, Anne Brown, Mrs.
Camomile, Glen
Camp, Bettie
Camp, Mildred
Camp, Virgil
Campbell, Aggie
Campbell, Annie
Campbell, Jay
Canepari, Ales
Cannon, Amelia
Cannon, E., Miss
Cannon, Elias M.
Cannon, Flora Mathews, Mrs.
Cannon, Frances
Cannon, Janath Russell
Cannon, Hester
Cannon, Ida
Cannon, Joseph
Cannon, Margaret S.
Cannon, Theodore L.
Cannon, Tracy Y.
Cannon, Victor E.
Cannon, W., Miss
Capson, Albert Maurice
Card, Elaine Anderson, Mrs.
Cardall, Lucile. *See* Beyer, Lucile
    Cardall
Careless, George Edward Percy
Careless, Lavinia
Carey, Beatrice, Mrs.
Carlisle, Thain
Carlson, Jean T., Mrs.
Carlson, Richard L.
Carlson, Suzanne Sanborn, Mrs.
Carr, Haven R.
Carson, Hazel
Carter, Bertha
Carter, Florence N., Mrs.
Carter, Hattie

Carter, Kathleen. *See* Boyd, Kathleen Carter
Carter, Wayne D.
Carver, Agnes V., Mrs.
Carway, Pamla
Case, Stephen T.
Castler, Mr.
Castleton, Charles
Castleton, David
Castleton, Grant A.
Castleton, John B.
Castleton, L. G. (Jerry)
Castleton, W. C.
Chace, Eunice
Chalmers, Jennie
Chamberlain, John H.
Chamberlain, Bessie
Chamberlain, Carrie
Chamberlain, Joseph
Chandler, Priscilla
Chandler, Rose
Chapman, June Pehrson, Mrs.
Chapman, Vernon
Chartrand, Joseph Pymm
Chartrand, Judith Baur, Mrs.
Chatelain, Richard N.
Chatfield, Val J., Mrs.
Chatterton, Carolyn S., Mrs.
Cheapella, Ollie Jean
Checketts, Myrtle. *See* Marsh, Myrtle Checketts
Cheesman, Millie Foster, Mrs.
Cheney, Mildred
Cheshire, James D., Jr.
Chester, J. H., Mrs.
Child, Ramon M.
Childs, Alta Victoria, Miss
Childs, Catherine
Chipman, Bertha
Chipman, Betty Jean Saville, Mrs.
Chipman, Davis H.
Chipman, Mildred
Chipman, Nan
Christensen, Augusta, Mrs.
Christensen, Clara
Christensen, Dorotha
Christensen, Ellen
Christensen, H. J.
Christensen, Harold
Christensen, Hugh W.
Christensen, Hy J. C.
Christensen, Jo Ann Williams
Christensen, Kate
Christensen, Lela G., Mrs.
Christensen, Lillie
Christensen, Marlene Hewlett, Mrs.
Christensen, Mary Ann Clyde, Mrs.
Christensen, Milton
Christensen, Opal
Christensen, Rudolph
Christensen, Shirley. *See* Eggington, Shirley Christensen
Christensen, William L.
Christenson, Patricia Jean Babb, Mrs.
Christholm, Joy Thalman, Mrs.
Christiansen, Frances
Christianson, Joseph
Christopher, Anna, Mrs.
Christopher, M. A., Mrs.
Christopher, Raymond
Christopherson, Dagmar
Christopherson, E.
Christopherson, Lamar S.
Christopherson, M.
Christopherson, M. E.
Chryst, Jewel
Chryst, Robert Vernon
Clapham, Charles
Clapham, Elizabeth
Clapham, George Herbert
Clapham, Gudrum Lillewick, Mrs.
Clark, Mrs.
Clark, Annie
Clark, Arvilla, Miss
Clark, Elayne Bright
Clark, Elmer
Clark, Estelle. *See* Stubbs, Estelle Clark
Clark, Grace

Clark, Helen E., Mrs.
Clark, Jacquetta Johnson
Clark, John
Clark, Joyce Murray, Mrs.
Clark, Karen
Clark, L. S.
Clark, L. W.
Clark, L. W.
Clark, Mary R.
Clark, Osborne
Clark, Owen
Clark, Percy G.
Clark, Ruel
Clark, VeAnn
Clark, Wynetta. *See* Martin, Wynetta Clark
Clarke, Louise Abegg, Mrs.
Clawson, Barbara. *See* Hewlett, Barbara Clawson
Clawson, Birdie. *See* Cummings, Birdie Clawson
Clawson, Evelyn
Clawson, Orin
Clawson, Patricia. *See* Redford, Patricia Clawson
Clawson, Ruth J., Mrs.
Clawson, S. H., Mrs.
Clawson, Sue
Clawson, Thoma
Clawson, Thomas A., Jr.
Clayton, Belle
Clayton, C. M.
Clayton, J. L.
Clayton, John L.
Clayton, Martha
Clayton, Maurice
Clayton, Patricia J.
Clayton, Robert E.
Clayton, Vera, Mrs.
Clayton, Vinnie
Clayton, Will
Clegg, Phyllis O. *See* Tucker, Phyllis Clegg
Clegg, Ruth
Clements, C. Roland
Clements, W. E.
Clinger, Richard
Clive, William C.
Clough, Susan Reed, Mrs.
Clyde, Mary Ann. *See* Christensen, Mary Ann Clyde
Coalter, Fergus
Cobb, J. Kent
Cobia, Raydell S., Mrs.
Cocking, Albert E.
Colbert, John S.
Colebrook, Nellie
Coleman, Ruth
Collett, Richard C.
Collier, Gwladys E. Morgan, Mrs.
Collier, Vernon
Collins, Sonya
Condie, Douglas
Condie, Gertrude
Condie, Jeanette. *See* Pearson, Jeanette Condie
Condie, Richard P.
Converse, May
Cook, Elease
Cook, Elsie
Cook, Janeece Cynthia Bush
Cook, John H.
Cook, Mary Ann
Cook, Patricia
Cook, Susan B., Mrs.
Cooke, Sarah A.
Coomans, Nellie, Mrs.
Coombs, Barbara
Coombs, Jesse R.
Coombs, Marian S.
Coon, Eldruna W., Mrs.
Cooper, Edna
Cooper, Emily. *See* Beezley, Emily Cooper
Cooper, Hattie, Mrs.
Cooper, Lizzie
Cooper, Mabel
Cope, Emma
Cope, F. W.
Copling, Wilfred O.

Coppin, Kathleen Butler
Corless, Edith
Cormay, Pamela
Cornwall, Allen
Cornwall, Bonnie
Cornwall, Joanne A.
Cornwall, Joseph Spencer
Cornwall, Marian
Cornwall, Mary H., Mrs.
Cornwall, Melvin C.
Cornwall, Millicent D., Mrs.
Cornwall, Oscar
Cornwall, Shirl
Cornwall, Shirley W.
Cottam, N. L., Mr.
Cottam, N. L., Mrs.
Cotton, Minerva
Coulam, H., Miss
Coult, Beulah Hinckley, Mrs.
Coulter, Fergus
Cowburn, R. H.
Cowley, Gae
Cowley, LaVon C.
Cox, Donna
Cox, Gaylen J.
Cox, William M.
Coy, Victor J.
Cram, Fay
Crandall, Don A.
Crawford, James
Crawford, Thomas C.
Crawford, Will
Critchlow, Frances
Critchlow, Patricia
Crocker, Edna G., Mrs.
Crofts, Connie Consoer, Mrs.
Crook, Ray John
Crookston, Eve, Mrs.
Cropper, Deon P., Mrs.
Crosby, Marcia V. *See* Green, Marcia Crosby
Cross, Ada
Crotch, Lily May, Miss
Crotch, William Ed.
Crow, La Rena, Miss
Crumpton, Emily
Cufflin, Vinnie
Culverwell, Pat, Mrs.
Cummings, Birdie Clawson
Cummings, Florence. *See* Youngberg, Florence Cummings
Cummings, Joye Jensen, Mrs.
Cummings, Mary Louise. *See* Swenson, Mary Louise Cummings
Cummock, Annie
Cummock, John B.
Cundick, Robert
Curtis, Dorothy
Curtis, Eldra or Elda W.
Curtis, Elsie or Ilse, Mrs.
Cushing, L., Miss
Cushing, Lilly
Cushing, Myrtle, Miss
Cutler, Jewel, Mrs.
Cutler, Lila B.
Cutler, Lucy
Cutler, Sue. *See* Liljegren, Sue Cutler
Czerny, Winfried

Dalby, Olive
Dalby, Francis F.
Dale, Maxine H.
Dalgleish, Hyrum C.
Dangerfield, Layne
Daniels, Alice
Dansie, Tasma, Mrs.
Danzig, Peter A.
Darger, Arlene B., Mrs.
Darger, Stanford P.
Darke, Yvonne
Darley, Roy Maughan
Darne, Della
Dastrup, D. Kent
Dastrup, Erva Dean, Mrs.
Dastrup, Kathleen McKee
Davenport, Calvin
Davenport, Ira
Davies, Dorothy, Miss

Davies, Henry
Davies, John
Davies, Marilyn. *See* Sirrine, Marilyn Davies
Davies, Morgan Alfred
Davis, Alice
Davis, Alice Stephens
Davis, Anita Hyatt
Davis, Blanche
Davis, Busly, Miss
Davis, Carol
Davis, Edward
Davis, Esther
Davis, Faye
Davis, Hannah
Davis, Hazel
Davis, Lotta or Lottie
Davis, Merlin
Davis, Pearl Kimball
Davis, Reed
Davis, Reid H.
Davis, Robert I
Davis, T.
Davis, Toni Rae, Mrs.
Davis, Vickie Lou Ungerman, Mrs.
Dawson, James
Day, Arthur
Day, W. Daniel
Daynes, Deila
Daynes, John
Daynes, Joseph J.
Daynes, Robert F.
Dean, Arden
Dean, Bessie
Dean, Leo A.
Dean, Lizette, Miss
Dean, William J.
Deane, Lucy
Debendiner, Leonore E.
DeBruin, Martine, Mrs.
Decker, Louisa Lees, Mrs.
Decker, Noram
Dedekind, Deborah C. *See* Romney, Deborah Dedekind
DeGooyer, John
DeGray, Selina
DeHaan, John Egbert
Dehlin, Eda
Delaney, Aleaha, Miss
DeLang or Delange, Cornelius
Dennison, Sarah I.
Den Ouden, Cornelis
Densley, Fred Earl
Derby, Richard
Deri, Ella
Derrick, F.
Derrickson, Frankie
DeSpain, Cleo
Despain, Gertrude
Devereaux, Wayne N.
DeYoung, Lewis Henry
Dick, Richard S.
Diehl, Margaret
Dietz, Conrad
Dill, Clive Lyon, Jr.
Dimmick, Merrill
Dinger, Marilyn Louise
Dinwoodey, Annette
Dinwoodey, Flora
Dittmer, Alma
Divett, Sam, Mrs.
Dixon, Crissie
Dixon, Dennis M.
Dock, Roger L.
Dodworth, Beatrice
Dodworth, G., Mrs.
Doezie, Girard
Doezie, Jacob
Donaldson, Carrie
Donaldson, Edna C.
Donaldson, G. Kent
Donaldson, Mamie
Donalson, Kathleen
Done, Irene
Done, Ivy
Done, Otto
Donelson, Earl
Donelson, Laura
Donelson, Richard
Dories, John

Dorius, R. E.
Dorius, R. Joel
Doty, Claudius
Doubleday, H., Mrs.
Doubleday, Henry
Doud, Harlan
Doud, Stella
Dougall, Hugh W.
Dowse, Julie F., Mrs.
Dowse, William E.
Doxey, William
Draney, Lois. See Phillips, Lois Draney
Draper, Melba
Drawe, Harold W.
Drews, Arnold O.
Driscoll, Shirley
Druce, Nellie. See Pugsley, Nellie Druce
Duckworth, James H.
Dudley, Joseph S.
Duersch, Fred, Jr.
Dummer, Valeen B., Mrs.
Dunbar, Eliza
Dunbar, James T.
Duncan, D.
Duncan, Homer
Duncan, Hortense Hinckly, Mrs.
Duncan, Ione, Miss
Duncan, Jean, Miss
Duncan, L. C., Mr.
Duncan, L. C., Mrs.
Duncan, LaMar
Duncomb, Leah Shindler, Mrs.
Dunford, M. Diane, Miss
Dunn, A., Miss
Dunn, Charlene Morr, Mrs.
Dunn, M., Miss
Dunn, Melvin W.
Dunn, Thomas, Jr.
Durrams, C. J.
Durrant, Ardelle. See Romney, Ardelle Durrant
Durrant, S. T.
Durrant, Vera
Dwyer, Kate
Dyer, George
Dyer, Mary S.
Dyer, May

Eames, Janine McBride, Mrs.
Eames, Oliver D.
Earll, Lizzie. See Lee, Lizzie Earll
Earnshaw, Hattie
Eastman, Betty Hyde
Easton, R. C.
Eberhart, Marjorie
Eccles, Albert, Sr.
Eccles, Albert, Jr.
Eccles, Caroline T., Mrs.
Eccles, Faye S., Mrs.
Eckard, Minnie
Eddington, Janet Whitman, Mrs.
Eddington, Louie
Eddington, Rose
Edholm, Charlina
Edmunds, Lizzie
Edwards, Craig M.
Edwards, Edna
Edwards, Lizzie Thomas, Mrs.
Edwards, Mae
Edwards, R., Miss
Egan, Dick H.
Egan, Doyle Carlos
Egan, L. M. W., Mrs.
Egan, Mary Jane
Egan, Shirley Peterson, Mrs.
Eggington, Donald R.
Eggington, Shirley, Mrs.
Egli, Susan N., Mrs.
Ekberg, Hildur M., Miss
Elggren, Olive Hickman Rich
Eliason, Leone H., Mrs.
Elieson, Clara, Miss
Elison, Marilyn
Elison, Rachael
Elkins, Alma
Elkins, John
Ellett, Billie Dean or Deen
Ellis, Alice

Ellis, James
Ellis, Robert J.
Ellis, Susan
Ellis, Suzanne
Ellison, Hazel, Mrs.
Ellsmore, Alice
Ellsmore, Ellen
Ellsmore, Emily
Ellsworth, Julia C.
Elzinga, John
Emery, George R.
Emery, H.
Ence, Dorothy. See Beck, Dorothy Ence
Enciso, Paul
Engberg, Vera
England, Breck (Richard)
English, Marie
Enniss, Jean G., Mrs.
Ensign, Albert
Ensign, Horace S., Jr.
Ensign, H. S., Mrs.
Ensign, Ivie J., Miss
Ensign, Martha J., Mrs.
Ensign, Rula
Epperson, Amos
Epperson, Amos, Mrs.
Erb, DeVere
Erickson, Carrie
Erickson, Florence C., Mrs.
Erickson (or Erekson), Margaret. See Monson, Margaret Erickson
Erickson, Yvonne. See Steiger, Yvonne
Erikson, Lettie
Eriksson, Herbert
Ernst, Justus
Ertmann, Mary Jane Pidd, Mrs.
Eskelson, LaMar C.
Espinosa, Vera Monson, Mrs.
Evans, Catherine. See Giles, Catherine Evans
Evans, Colleen
Evans, David William
Evans, Edna, Miss
Evans, Elizabeth
Evans, George D.
Evans, Georgia Kanell, Mrs.
Evans, H. T.
Evans, Ivy
Evans, Jessie
Evans, Jessie. See Smith, Jessie Evans
Evans, Joanne
Evans, John
Evans, Lynn B.
Evans, Oakley S.
Evans, Paul H.
Evans, Richard L.
Evans, T. Max
Eves, Arthur G., Jr.

Fairbanks, Craig
Fairbanks, Fonda Williams, Mrs.
Fairbanks, Ortho
Fairbanks, Reed S.
Fallows, Albert D.
Fallows, Lorna Lowry, Mrs.
Fallows, Tom
Fanning, Jane
Farley, Brent
Farley, Janene
Farnsberg, Elsie
Farnsworth, Dean
Farnsworth, Karl
Farnsworth, Ovid L
Farrell, Alice C.
Faux, Annette
Fechser, Kenneth
Felt, C. B.
Felt, D.
Felt, Harry
Felt, Lizzie
Felt, Minnie
Felt, Richard N.
Fenn, Nancy Duffie Furner, Mrs.
Fenton, Wanda H., Mrs.
Ferguson, George C.
Fergerson, Mary E. Sherriff, Mrs.
Fernley, Annette B., Mrs.

Fernley, Edward R.
Fernstrom, Dolores Seal
Ferre, Loren W.
Ferre, LuCretia
Ferrell, Dennis M.
Ferrell, Desna
Ferrin, May
Ferrin, Minnie
Fetzer, Richard W.
Fife, Florence
Fillmore, David P.
Fineshriber, Marilynn Kay Pitts, Mrs.
Finlinson, Luella Wheeler, Mrs.
Fisher, Donna
Fisher, E. W.
Fisher, Jon E.
Fisher, Lon
Fisher, Marianne C., Mrs.
Fisher, Merlin
Fisher, Robert S.
Fitzgerald, Judith
Fitzgerald, Michael
Flanders, Twylla Gibb, Mrs.
Flandro, Beverly
Flashman, Rose Edith
Flemming, Betty
Flinders, Leland E.
Foerstl, Eleanor
Fogelberg, S. W.
Fogg, Cheryl
Folkerson, Laura
Folsom, Robert E.
Fonnesbeck, Luna, Miss
Forback, Ludwig
Forbush, Mary E.
Ford, Jacquiln
Forman, Nellie G.
Forsha, Douglass
Fortie, J. A.
Foster, Alice
Foster, Aurelia
Foster, Charles E.
Foster, Doreen Lander
Foster, Frank
Foster, George
Foster, Millie
Foster, William H.
Foulger, Josephene C., Mrs.
Foulger, Paul A.
Fowler, Annie
Fowler, Esther
Fowler, James
Fox, Ann Schlofman, Mrs.
Fox, Joan Ellen Anderson, Mrs.
Fox, Lillian Stokes, Mrs.
Fox, Lucy Grant, Mrs.
Fox, Wallace
Fraenkel, Jean B., Mrs.
Frampton, Delight Thomas, Mrs.
Francom, Elva
Franzen, Christine
Fraseur, Bluford, Mrs.
Fredrickson, Clara, Mrs.
Freeburn, Archie
Freed, Edward
Freeman, Nan
Freeman, Ray
Freeze, George
Freeze, M., Miss
French, Jacqueline
Frisby, H. LeRoy
Frisby, Orlene, Mrs.
Frisby, Stella. See Miller, Stella Frisby
Froisland, M.
Frost, Frank
Frost, Nettie
Frost, Mathilda P.
Frost, Rosalie Richards, Mrs.
Fuller, F. C.
Fuller, Fred
Fuller, Lael J., Mrs.
Fuller, Marvin
Fuller, Nida
Fullmer, Gladys. See Pixton, Gladys Fullmer
Fullmer, Jeanette, Mrs.
Fullmer, Maude Stephens
Fullmer, Valetta

Fulmer, H.
Fulmer, J. M.
Fulmer, Minnie
Furner, Duffie. See Fenn, Duffie Furner
Furner, George T.
Furness, Emma Ellen Alder, Mrs.
Fyans, Joe

Gagon, Lulu
Galbraith, Lela, Mrs.
Gale, A. LeRoy
Gale, Ella, Mrs.
Gale, Jennie
Gallagher, James
Gallegos, Renee
Gallup, Virginia S.
Garbe, Louise
Gardiner, Althea H.
Gardiner, Amy H.
Gardiner, Henry
Gardner, Aleen A.
Gardner, Boneta
Gardner, Claribel
Gardner, Cora S., Mrs.
Gardner, Karma
Gardner, Olga Helen Dotson, Mrs.
Gardner, Sally Louise, Mrs.
Garff, DeVal R.
Garff, Herschal V.
Garner, Ellen
Garner, Violet, Mrs.
Garrard, V. Gwen
Gasser, Anna B., Miss
Gasser, Freda Nadine (Freddie), Mrs.
Gates, Brigham Cecil
Geddes, Mrs.
Gedge, Charlotte
Gedge, Margaret A.
Gee, Kenneth V.
Geis, Gustave A.
George, Floyd Blaine
Gerrard, Bertha
Gerstner, Marvin D.
Gibb, Twylla. See Flanders, Twylla Gibb
Gibbons, Carolyn Sue
Gibbons, LeRoy, III
Gibbons, Mildred, Mrs.
Gibbs, W. Sherman
Gilbert, James
Giles, Allen R.
Giles, Catherine Evans
Giles, Georgeva. See Morgan, Georgeva Giles
Giles, Henry E.
Giles, Hyrum
Giles, Linda
Giles, Merle
Giles, Sarah Hague
Giles, Sybil, Mrs.
Gill, K.
Gillespie, E., Mrs.
Gillespie, Moroni B.
Gillies, Irene
Gillies, Jessie
Glade, George L.
Glade, Virginia
Glenn, J. W.
Glissmeyer, August
Glissmeyer, Darro H.
Glissmeyer, Henry A.
Goddard, Benjamin
Goddard, Harold W.
Goddard, Jeanne King, Mrs.
Goddard, Stephen
Godfrey, Elaine, Mrs.
Godfrey, C. Joseph
Godwin, Emma S.
Gold, Elmina
Gold, Nicholas B.
Gold, Ruth Everton
Gonzales, Jane Meyerhoffer, Mrs.
Gonzales, Rolando G.
Goodman, Thomas
Goodyear, Hyrum
Goodyear, Lucille
Gore, Sherry Sue
Gorring, Hortence

Goss, Charlotte
Goss, Frederick
Goss, Louise
Gotberg, Edna
Gottfredson, Don M.
Gourley, Opal
Graham, Fred C.
Grange, William
Granger, Hazel, Mrs.
Granger, Beryl
Grant, Catherine H., Mrs.
Grant, Minerva Unice, Mrs.
Grant, Patricia S., Mrs.
Grant, Richard G.
Graves, Lanette Robinson, Mrs.
Gray, Andrew S.
Gray, Blossom N.
Gray, G. R.
Gray, Jessie
Grayston, Ida. See Tomlison, Ida
  Grayston
Greaves, William Lloyd
Greeff, Jacob
Green, Arnold Cornell
Green, William H., Jr
Green, F. W.
Green, John Fredrick
Green, Lizzie
Green, Marcia Vowles Crosby,
  Mrs.
Green, May
Green, Norma
Green, R. N., Mrs.
Green, Susan
Green, Vivian
Greene, Norma
Greenhalgh, Betty
Gregory, Herold L. (Huck)
Gregory, Joanna
Gregory, Kate
Grieve, Jessie Ellen
Grieve, Thomasina
Griffin, J. Marcus
Griffiths, Lizzie. See Holmes, Lizzie
  Griffiths
Griffiths, Marian C.
Griggs, Thomas C.
Groesbeck, Kate
Gronemann, Thomas
Groo, Whitney
Gross, Charles T.
Grossberg, Aaron
Grover, Linda Elaine
Grover, Marilyn
Grow, Emily S.
Grow, Henry
Grow, Joseph H.
Grow, Robert M.
Grow, Sarah
Grubbs, Helen DuBell Patten, Mrs.
Gudmundsen, Sydney L. See Pike,
  Sydney Gudmundsen
Gulbransen, Norman
Gundersen, Esther Luella (Lou) Van
  Dam, Mrs.
Gundersen, Had B.
Gunderson, George D.
Gunderson, Ruby Brown
Gunn, Fanny Louise
Gunn, J. T.
Gutke, Nellie
Gygi, Lola
Gygi, Ruth

Haag, R. T.
Haddock, Mollie
Haddock, Sarah
Haertel, Erich P.
Hague, Sarah. See Giles, Sarah
  Hague
Hale, Cleve
Hales, Ronald Thane
Halgren, Joseph D.
Hall, Hazel
Hall, Jeni
Hall, Mina
Hall, Saundra Whipple, Mrs.
Halliday, John R.
Halliday, Nina
Halsett, Josie

Halsett, Ruth W.
Halvorsen, Edna MarGene Poul-
  son, Mrs.
Halverson, Deoine
Halverson, Dorothy
Halverson, Joseph
Halverson, Ray
Hamilton, Barry
Hamilton, Elna
Hammond, Calder
Hammond, Martha
Hammond, Richard Mardell
Hampton, Zora W., Mrs.
Hamson, Marcus Lee
Hand, J. T.
Hanks, Jean Palmer, Mrs.
Hanks, Paul A.
Hannabell, D., Miss
Hansen, Aaron A.
Hansen, Donna M. Kowallis, Mrs.
Hansen, F. Kent
Hansen, Francelle B.
Hansen, Golden K.
Hansen, Hans W.
Hansen, Kenneth Lee
Hansen, Lola
Hansen, Maurine
Hansen, Robert N.
Hansen, Roma
Hansen, Walter H.
Hantz, K.
Harder, Virginia
Hardman, Betty
Hardy, Esther Margetts
Hardy, Kenneth J.
Hardy, Lena
Hardy, O. F., Miss
Hardy, Roy L.
Harker, Ray
Harline, Ida
Harlow, Ardythe Twitchell, Mrs.
Harper, Lester John
Harrington, Ione Lunt, Mrs.
Harris, Clinton
Harris, Colleen R.
Harris, DeLora
Harris, Edith
Harris, Freda Henrie, Mrs.
Harris, Gaylen
Harris, H. Jarolde
Harris, Lillian W.
Harris, M., Miss
Harris, Preston
Harris, Richard Carl
Harrison, Conrad B.
Harrison, Edith
Harrison, T.
Harston, Richard
Hart, Camille, Mrs.
Hartvigsen, Janice Beesley, Mrs.
Harvatin, Lila. See Anderton,
  Lila H.
Haslam, Emma
Haslam, James E.
Hassell, Cora Beth
Hassell, Myrth, Mrs.
Hatch, Luacine
Hawkes, Earl Rich
Hawkes, Pricilla
Hawkins, Dale
Hawkins, Lucille
Hawkins, Merrill G.
Hawley, Nettie
Haymond, Marie
Hazen, Ida
Headman, Melvin
Heath, Luella Sharp
Heath, Sasie
Hebdon, Bonnie. See White, Bon-
  nie Hebdon
Hebdon, Geraldine
Heder, Diane. See Beesley, Diane
  Heder
Heesche, Kate
Heim, Edith Adamson
Heiner, Gary Lee
Heiner, Laura Shand, Mrs.
Heiniger, Lydia
Hellier, John Walter
Helme, Clyde O.

Hendersen, Mark Artie
Henderson, Bonnie Cornwall, Mrs.
Henderson, Eva. See Bettridge, Eva
  May H.
Henderson, Lany. See Langton,
  Lany Henderson
Hendrickson, Dorothy Kennard
Hendrickson, Oscar J.
Hendry, Lizzie
Henry, John M.
Heppler, Mary, Miss
Hepworth, Ida, Mrs.
Herbst, John R.
Hess, Marjorie
Hess, Susan
Hewlett, Barbara Clawson, Mrs.
Hewlett, Charles
Hewlett, Lester F.
Hewlett, Margaret S., Mrs.
Hewlett, Peggy Brazier, Mrs.
Heywood, Kittie
Heywood, L. L., Miss
Hibbard, John C.
Hibben, Gilbert W.
Hicks, Eunice S., Mrs.
Hicken, Ward M
Hickenlooper, George
Hickison, Wilfrid L.
Hickman, F. L.
Hickman, Olive N. See Rich, Olive
  Hickman
Hiebert, Judy Linn
Higgins, Mr.
Higgins, H. D.
Higgins, Elsie, Mrs.
Higgins, Rowland
Higginson, R. Keith
Higgs, Lucile Child, Mrs.
Hight, Wallace E.
Higley, Pamela Van Brocklin, Mrs.
Hildreth, Gailya B., Mrs.
Hill, Derylis. See Bush, Derylis Hill
Hill, Edna M.
Hill, Edythe or Edith F.
Hill, Flora Shipp
Hill, H. S.
Hill, J. Dean
Hill, Joseph S.
Hill, Marlin V.
Hill, Ruland
Hillier, Helen Russell, Mrs.
Hillstead, E., Miss
Hillstead, James
Hinckley, Afton
Hinckley, Reulah. See Coult, Beu-
  lah Hinckley
Hinckley, Clara
Hinckley, Edith
Hinckley, Ira
Hinckley, Josie
Hinckley, Lee
Hinckley, Wave, Mrs.
Hirsh, Elizabeth R.
Hisatake, Thelma M.
Hobson, May L.
Hodge, R. H.
Hoel, Jennie H., Mrs.
Hoff, Laura
Hoffhiens, Gerald A.
Hoffman, Lena
Hoffman, Marie
Hogensen, Esther. See Holbrook,
  Esther Hogensen
Hogensen, H. J.
Hogensen, Johanna
Hogenson, Julia, Miss
Hogge, Elmer M.
Holbrook, Alice
Holbrook, Esther Hogensen, Mrs.
Holbrook, Everett
Holbrook, Robert B.
Holdaway, Loren D.
Holdiway, (Holding) W. S.
Holladay, Joy
Holland, Ann
Holliday, George T.
Hollingsworth, Martha
Holmes, Annie
Holmes, Elizabeth Griffiths, Mrs.
Holmes, Hannah

Holmes, J., Miss
Holmes, John
Holmes, John L.
Holmes, Samuel
Holmes, Sophie
Holmes, Tecla
Holsett, Josie
Holyoak, Joseph J.
Holyoak, Veneeta
Homer, Gerald Lynn
Hoofer, Louise
Hook, A. W.
Hook, Ernest E.
Hooper, Carolyn
Hooper, Emily
Hooper, Helen P., Mrs.
Hooper, Thomas A.
Hoover, G. W. (Bill)
Hopewell, M. J., Miss
Hopkins, Myriel Cluff
Hoppie, Barbara See Brimley, Bar-
  bara H.
Hoppie, Joan. See Ogden, Joan H.
Horne, Clara
Horne, Grant
Horne, Laura
Horne, Mattie. See Tingey, Mattie
  Horne
Horne, Minnie. See Jones, Minnie
  Horne
Horne, Virginia, Miss
Horne, W. P.
Horsley, Adelina
Horsley, Amy
Horsley, T. W.
Houtz, Kate
Hovey, Lester D.
Howard, Stephen T.
Howard, Thomas
Howard, Virginia S.
Howarth, Alice
Howell, Kathryn Ann. See Ruther-
  ford, Kathryn Ann H.
Howell, W.
Howells, Mary Peirce, Mrs.
Hoyt, Barbara I.
Hsieh, Susan Ying-Chi
Hsueh, Helen Lee (Schueh-Mei)
Hubbard, J., Miss
Hubbard, L. A., Miss
Hubbard, Layne
Huber, Barbara Ann
Hutt, Dolores
Huff, Lora Lee
Hughes, David
Hughes, Gary W.
Hulbert, A.
Hulbert, Gertie
Hulbert, Minnie
Hulet, Vivian
Hull, Maggie C.
Hull, Thomas
Humphries, Lee
Humphreys, Marilyn
Hunsaker, Bertha M., Mrs.
Hunsaker, Elmer
Hunsaker, Mary Stewart, Mrs.
Hunter, Jeanne C., Mrs.
Huntsman, Delta
Huntsman, Ned
Hurst, Cecelia Jackson, Mrs.
Hurst, James
Hurst, Leland
Hurtado, Victor A.
Hyatt, Anita. See Davis, Anita
  Hyatt
Hyde, Betty Ivins. See Eastman,
  Betty Hyde
Hyde, E., Miss
Hyde, J. W.
Hyde, J. W., Mrs.
Hymas, Max

Ingalls, Max
Ingalls, Virginia Duncan, Mrs.
Ipson, D. P.
Ipson, Joseph Jared
Ipson, Powell
Ipson, Virginia G., Mrs.
Irvine, Esther, Miss

193

Nelson, V. Rene
Nelson, Victor J.
Nelson, Zora B., Mrs.
Nesbitt, Thomas
Neslin, Nellie
Ness, Blossom
Ness, Raynor
Nettleton, C. J.
Neuhart, Edna Lyle Jenkins, Mrs.
Neve, A., Miss
Newbold, Reed C.
Newey, Joseph M.
Newman, Ada C., Mrs.
Newman, Colleen
Newman, Laurel Kay Kawk
Newren, Leslie S.
Newren, Loeto Y. (Loey)
Newren, Louise Brown, Mrs.
Newsom, May
Newsome, Donald W.
Newton, Lizzie Parker
Newton, S. E., Miss
Nichols, E. H.
Nichols, Maxine
Nielsen, Carol Anne
Nielsen, Julia Ann
Nielsen, Lee
Nielson, Evelyn
Nielson, John Marlowe
Nielson, Lorna
Nielson, Marlin A.
Nielson, Mary Schindler, Mrs.
Nielson, Malva, Mrs.
Nielson, Verda, Mrs.
Nilson, Elsie. See Jones, Elsie Nilson
Nilsson, Alfred
Nilsson, Ray F.
Nilsson, Wilford
Nixon, Myrene Kemp, Mrs.
Noall, Claire
Noall, Ethel
Noall, Harold
Noall, Ivy B.
Noall, Matthew
Noble, Wallace Ray
Noe, Lynden R.
Nooley, William R., Jr.
Norbe, Christine
Nordberg, A. C.
Nordberg, Elsie Harline
Nordfelt, Desna Ferrell, Mrs.
Norman, Ida, Miss
Norman, Jess Roger
Norman, Keith E.
Noyes, Celeste
Noyes, David W.
Noyes, Jan Camp, Mrs.
Noyes, Lucian L.
Nyberg, Jean, Mrs.
Nylander, Axel A.

Oakden, Donal Ray
Oastle, Burke
Oborne, Annie May, Mrs.
Ockey, Sharon Brimley, Mrs.
Odell, Christine, Miss
Odell, Sharon Faye. See Burt, Sharon Odell
O'Donnal, Melvin C.
Ofgreen, Pearl
Ogaard, Enid Nelson, Mrs.
Ogden, Joan Hoppie, Mrs.
Ogden, Larry Wayne
Ogden, Scott
Oldroyd, Hannah L.
Olsen, Agnes. See Thomas, Agnes Olsen
Olsen, Annie
Olsen, Birdie
Olsen, Effie
Olsen, Hyrum
Olsen, J. J.
Olsen, Lettie
Olsen, Orrin J.
Olsen, Sarah E. See Langford, Sarah E. Olsen
Olsen, Wanda S. Young, Mrs.
Olsen, Lois. See Beach, Lois Olson
Omer, Cherie Park, Mrs.

Openshaw, Lizzie
Openshaw, Mary
Orahood, Margaret
Orgill, Amy
Orullian, Joseph J.
Osborne, Nelson
Osguthorpe, Iva Russell, Mrs.
Osguthorpe, Lolly Sedgwick, Mrs.
Osguthorpe, Russell Trent
Oslett, Julie Ann
Osmond, Stephen D.
Ostler, Fanny
Ostler, O. R.
Ottinger, Helen
Ottley, Earl
Ottley, JoAnn S., Mrs.
Ottley, Jerold Don
Overlade, A. R.
Overson, Peter M.
Owen, Alvia C.
Owen, John L.
Owen, William D.
Owens, Hazel
Owens, Rial S.
Oyler, Kathy

Pace, Dorothy. See Pratt, Dorothy Pace
Pace, Gordon Arnold
Pace, Laura May Richards, Mrs.
Pack, Onita
Pack, M. E.
Pack, Wallace Dean
Pack, Ward E.
Packard, Clarence F.
Packard, Jane, Miss
Packard, Janet Dee. See Miller, Janet Packard
Packard, Lela
Padgen, May
Page, Lillie
Page, Marian W., Mrs.
Paine, Minnie
Palfreyman, Helen. See LeeMaster, Helen Palfreyman
Palmer, Annie
Palmer, Jean. See Hanks, Jean Palmer
Palmer, Sarah
Papworth, Ruth Wilcox, Mrs.
Pardoe, Florence
Pardoe, Isabella Brizzee, Mrs.
Pardoe, William
Park, Berniece
Park, John
Park, William
Park, William L., Jr.
Parker, Audrey M., Mrs.
Parker, Barbara Jean Gunn, Mrs.
Parker, Grace. See Taylor, Grace Parker
Parker, Lizzie
Parks, Jane R., Miss
Parks, Peggy Jane
Parrish, John
Parry, Dick
Parry, Dorothy Reid
Parry, E. F.
Parry, Edward
Parry, George
Parry, Georgia, Mrs.
Parry, Janet. See Broadbent, Janet Parry
Parry, John
Parry, Verna Monsen, Mrs.
Parsons, Arthur
Partridge, M. Olive, Mrs.
Passey, Violet P.
Patchel, Sue
Patrick, Carrie Thorne
Patrick, Lizzie
Patten, Helen DuBell. See Grubbs, Helen P.
Patten, W.
Patterson, Leila Bixby
Patterson, Patricia
Paul, Ivy
Paulsen, Bonnie Anderson, Mrs.
Peacock, Clara

Pearce, Kelly Thayne
Pearce, Mary Lynn. See Baddley, Mary Lynn Pearce
Pearson, Jeanette Condie, Mrs.
Pearson, Karl Lorenz
Pearson, Beverly Ostler, Mrs.
Pearson, Owen B.
Pearson, Stewart E.
Peart, A. Byron
Peck, Edna H., Mrs.
Pedersen, Annie
Pedersen, H. Robert
Pedersen, Jennie
Pehrson, June. See Chapman, June Pehrson
Pendleton, Erma
Pendleton, Laura Lee
Pendleton, Virginia
Penrose, Ettie
Penrose, Katie
Penrose, Marjorie, Miss
Penrose, Nellie
Peo, Jeffrey R.
Perkins, Helen
Perry, Hazel S.
Petersen, Gerald A.
Petersen, Nora
Petersen, P. Melvin
Petersen, Robert K.
Petersen, Thora
Peterson, A. F.
Peterson, A. W.
Peterson, Andrew
Peterson, Annie
Peterson, Brent R.
Peterson, Carolyn Faye, Miss
Peterson, Ebba
Peterson, Ellen H.
Peterson, Ervin
Peterson, Ethel, Mrs.
Peterson, Ervin
Peterson, Ferdinand
Peterson, Gertie
Peterson, Gunnel
Peterson, Hilma
Peterson, Melvin
Peterson, Minnie V. T.
Peterson, Rilla Wilson, Mrs.
Peterson, Virginia Isakson, Mrs.
Peterson, Wayne
Pettit, Katie
Pettit, Myrtle
Pexton, Richard N.
Pexton, Ronald D.
Phillips, J., Miss
Phillips, Lois Draney
Phillips, Raymond A.
Phillips, S. R.
Phillips, Sid
Pickett, Charles
Picco, Josephine
Picco, Lucy
Pidd, Dorothy
Pidd, Harry B.
Pidd, Mary Jane. See Ertmann, Mary Jane Pidd
Pierce, Eli
Pierce, Ida
Pierce, L. S., Miss
Pierce, Ramona
Piercy, Anna
Piesonotzki, Frieda
Pike, Kathleen
Pike, Malcolm Davis
Pike, Malcolm England
Pike, Sydney Gudmundsen, Mrs.
Pingree, George C.
Pinkerman, James K.
Pinkerton, Thomas G.
Pinney, Alice
Pinney, Josephine
Pitt, Ida
Pitts, Florence C.
Pitts, Marilyn. See Fineshriber, Marilyn P.
Pixton, Gladys Fullmer, Mrs.
Pixton, Thelma
Place, Doreen
Platt, Alonzo

Platt, Carlene O.
Platt, Daniel
Platt, Edward O.
Platt, Irene B.
Plouzek, Linda Simper, Mrs.
Plowgian, Marilyn Joy, Miss
Pocock, Norma R.
Poecker, Elfriede, Mrs.
Politonicz, Nona, Miss
Poll, Joseph
Poole, Peninah (Nina) W., Mrs.
Poole, Stanley S.
Porath, Shirley
Porter, D. LaMar
Porter, Earl C.
Porter, Elsie
Porter, Lyman Karl
Potter, Genevieve
Potter, Robert S.
Poulsen, Udell E.
Poulson, Alton Monte
Poulson, Florence K.
Poulter, W. Howard
Poulter, William I., Jr.
Poulton, Annie
Poulton, Florence
Poulton, J. T.
Poulton, James H.
Poulton, Louisa
Poulton, Walter J.
Poulton, William
Powell, Clarnell B.
Powell, Debra Ann
Powell, John
Prather, Loren John
Pratt, C. R.
Pratt, Calvin D.
Pratt, Donald Y.
Pratt, Dorothy Pace, Mrs.
Pratt, Irvine T.
Pratt, Margaret
Pratt, Marilyn Innes, Mrs.
Pratt, Marintha
Pratt, Maude E.
Pratt, Michael S.
Pratt, Neva
Pratt, Orson, Jr.
Pratt, P. O.
Pratt, Parley P.
Pratt, Percy W.
Pratt, Viola
Pratt, Winnie
Preece, Inez
Preece, Marjorie
Preston, Kate
Preston, May
Price, Mary
Priestly, Grace
Prince, Robert Scott
Provost, Beverly Smith
Provost, Sterling R.
Prows, Florence Stevens, Mrs.
Prows, Joseph H.
Prows, Joseph H., Jr.
Prows, Ronald S.
Pugsley, Nellie Druce, Mrs.
Pulley, Carol Rose. See Meyer, Carol Pulley
Pusey, Elaine W., Mrs.
Putnam, Martha
Pyper, Alex
Pyper, Emma
Pyper, George D.
Pyper, James M.
Pyper, Paul G.
Pyper, Ross

Quigley, Gordon M.
Quigley, L. Glen
Quillian, Joseph H.

Raleigh, Nettie
Ramsay, Marilyn
Rand, Emma
Randall, Beryl A., Miss
Rankin, Mary
Ransom, Jane
Ransom, Phyllis. See Madsen, Phyllis Ransom

Sitine, James
Skolfield, Jennie
Slight, Glen
Slighting, Adrian M.
Sloan, Betty Ellison, Mrs.
Slotboom, Marjorie B. Simons
Smith, A., Mrs.
Smith, A. F.
Smith, Adelaid
Smith, Albert
Smith, Amy
Smith, Arlene Ridges, Mrs.
Smith, Andrew
Smith, Angie
Smith, Bessie
Smith, Beth
Smith, Beverly. *See* Provost, Beverly Smith
Smith, Bona Bell
Smith, Charles
Smith, Cornelius, Jr.
Smith, D., Miss
Smith, Daphne
Smith, David A.
Smith, Donnetta O.
Smith, Earl
Smith, Edith
Smith, Edith Ball, Mrs.
Smith, Eliza James
Smith, Emmeret C.
Smith, Felice Swain
Smith, Florence C.
Smith, George C.
Smith, George H.
Smith, George O.
Smith, Gertrude S., Mrs.
Smith, H. J.
Smith, Hyrum M.
Smith, J., Miss
Smith, J. C.
Smith, J. G.
Smith, J. S.
Smith, Jennie
Smith, Jessie Evans, Mrs.
Smith, John H.
Smith, John J. (Jack)
Smith, John Y.
Smith, Joseph Fielding
Smith, L., Miss
Smith, Laura Nebeker
Smith, Leon G.
Smith, Lizzie
Smith, Lyla J.
Smith, Lorenzo
Smith, M. L., Miss
Smith, Manassa
Smith, Marilyn Yuille
Smith, Margine Ann
Smith, Marie
Smith, Mary A.
Smith, Mary F.
Smith, Mattie G.
Smith, Maude M., Miss
Smith, Millie
Smith, Minnie, Mrs.
Smith, Naomie
Smith, Robert
Smith, Robert E.
Smith, Robert W.
Smith, Sarah
Smith, Sue
Smith, Susie W.
Smith, Sylvia Dean
Smith, Vickey
Smith, Vilate. *See* Arnold, Vilate Smith
Smith, Wilma. *See* Kern, Wilma Smith
Smith, Wilma Gay. *See* Livsey, Wilma Smith
Smith, Winslow
Smithen, Rose E.
Smithies, James
Smurthwaite, Rhea Folsom, Mrs.
Smythe, A.C.
Snelgrove, E.S.
Snell, Claire
Snell, H.Y., Miss
Snell, Nettie
Snow, Barbara, Miss

Snow, Deneice
Snow, Helen
Solomon, Nellie
Solomon, Rosetta C.
Sonntag, Norma Kay, Mrs.
Sorensen, Clifford
Sorensen, Frederick C.
Sorensen, Jon Craig
Sorensen, Lillie
Sorensen, Marvin A.
Sorensen, Richard Scott
Sorenson, C.R.
Sorenson, John
Sorenson, M., Miss
Sorenson, Mattie
Sorenson, Paul
Southwick, Albert J.
Spall, Florence, Miss
Speer, Haru Jane. *See* Bromley, Haru Jane Speer
Spencer, Bertha C., Mrs.
Spencer, Bessie
Spencer, Cora
Spencer, Ed
Spencer, Katie
Spencer, Maitland G.
Spendlove, Marjorie Mower, Mrs.
Spendlove, Vaughn D.
Sperry, Annie
Sperry, Arthur
Sperry, H.
Sperry, M., Miss
Sperry, W.A.
Spilker, Christa D., Mrs.
Spry, Andrew
Spry, Gussie
Spry, Samuel
Squires, Carolyn Matthews, Mrs.
Squires, Glacia
Squires, Mary Rhodes, Mrs.
Squires, Victoria
Stahl, Margaret, Miss
Stallings, Tonia. *See* Jensen, Tonia Stallings
Stam, LaVern
Standing, Susan. *See* Rideout, Susan Standing
Stanford, Melvin Joseph
Stanley, Leola
Steadman, Calvin M.
Steadman, G. Valarie Hancock, Mrs.
Steadman, Kim Stanley
Steadman, Meade
Steadman, Stanley Glen
Steckler, F. Wayne
Steed, Della McAnne
Steiber, Merle
Steiger, Jerry R.
Steiger, Yvonne Marler Erickson, Mrs.
Steiner, Arles K.
Steiner, Elda Neves, Mrs.
Steiner, Thelma (Penny) Brown Singleton, Mrs.
Stenacher, Marie H.
Steorts, Gerald Glen
Stephens, Alice
Stephens, Esther D.
Stephens, Evan
Stephens, Maude. *See* Fullmer, Maude S.
Stephens, Sybil C.
Stephens, Wade N.
Sterling, Marie Diane
Stevens, Grayce Needham, Mrs.
Stevens, Orvilla Allred, Mrs.
Stevens, Robert
Stevens, Robert K.
Stevens, Ruth Lang, Mrs.
Stevensen, C.J.
Stevenson, E.
Stevenson, Hilda C., Mrs.
Stevenson, Lizzie
Stewart, Elaine McRae
Stewart, Irene
Stewart, Isaac M.
Stewart, Katherine Romney, Mrs.
Stewart, Lottie E.
Stewart, Mary Jane

Stewart, Mayda, Miss
Stewart, Robert
Stewart, Vera, Miss
Stobbe, Marie H.
Stoddard, Francis
Stoddard, Ruth Swensen
Stoker, Barbara Green, Mrs.
Stoker, Douglas G.
Stoker, Stephen G.
Stokes, Claudia. *See* Thurman, Claudia
Stokes, Lillian. *See* Fox, Lillian Stokes
Stokes, Terry Lynn
Stolk, Marjory L.
Stone, Shirley. *See* Storrs, Shirley Stone
Stoneman, Ena
Stoneman, Jamesina Bannatine, Mrs.
Stoneman, William Harper
Storrs, Margaret S. Jirovec, Mrs.
Storrs, Norven L.
Storrs, Richard
Storrs, Shirley Stone
Stout, Agnes
Stout, Alta, Miss
Stout, Inez. *See* Whipple, Inez Stout
Stout, Kathleen McDonald, Mrs.
Stout, L. Woodruff
Strand, LeRoy
Strehl, W. R.
Stringham, Bruce
Stringham, Dell B.
Stringham, Richard B.
Stromberg, Annie
Stromberg, Nellie
Stuart, Roy Lee
Stubbs, Estella Clark, Mrs.
Sudbury, Miss
Sudbury, Beverly, Mrs.
Sudbury, Don C.
Sudweeks, Virginia
Sugden, Frances. *See* Vane, Frances S.
Sullivan, Kristy Western, Mrs.
Summerhays, Beth P.
Summerhays, C.E.
Summerhays, J. Terry
Summerhays, Joseph R.
Summerhays, Lillian
Summerhays, Margaret
Summerhays, Mayme
Summers, Carol Ann. *See* Lee, Carol Ann Summers
Summers, Marian Taylor, Mrs.
Sundall, Leonora
Sundberg, Kathlyn
Sutton, Dorothy
Swain, A.R.
Swain, Felice
Swan, Emma
Swan, Verna. *See* Johnson, Verna Swan
Sweeten, Robert L.
Swensen, Alice Folland, Mrs.
Swensen, Karl Jones
Swensen, Ruth. *See* Stoddard, Ruth S.
Swenson, Annie
Swenson, Mary Louise Cummings, Mrs.
Swenson, Shirley Salm, Mrs.
Swenson, Vernie C.
Swift, J., Miss

Tadje, Freda
Taggart, Blanche M., Mrs.
Taggart, Scott
Taggart, Susan Linda
Tak, Hendrik W.
Tame, Shirley. *See* Reynolds, Shirley Tame
Tanner, Marilyn
Tanner, ValEen
Tarbox, Lewis
Tate, Joyce. *See* Wilcox, Joyce Tate
Tate, Suzanne Jeppson, Mrs.
Taylor, Carolyn, Miss

Taylor, Dawn L. Pratt, Mrs.
Taylor, Eleanor
Taylor, Ethel
Taylor, Florence
Taylor, Gloria B., Mrs.
Taylor, Grace Parker, Mrs.
Taylor, J.H., Miss
Taylor, Jabez
Taylor, John
Taylor, Kate
Taylor, Katherine Kelly
Taylor, Lizzie
Taylor, Mamie
Taylor, Marvin R.
Taylor, Norman L.
Taylor, Ralph R.
Taylor, Richard M.
Taylor, Robert
Taylor, Ruby
Taylor, Sarah H.
Tayner, A., Miss
Teeples, Verl
Teerlink, Evelyn
Teerlink, Marie
Tenney, Patricia. *See* Larsen, Patricia Tenney
Terry, Elvis B.
Terry, Isabella A.
Tester, M.A.
Teuscher, Clara
Thalman, Joy Mimi. *See* Christholm, Joy T.
Thatcher, Fanny Young, Mrs.
Thayne, David C.
Theurer, Berenice Steele, Mrs.
Thiriot, Rhea S., Mrs.
Thomas, Agnes O.
Thomas, Agnes
Thomas, Charles J.
Thomas, Claire
Thomas, Delano
Thomas, Delight. *See* Frampton, Delight T.
Thomas, Ellen
Thomas, Emma Lindsay, Mrs.
Thomas, Evangeline
Thomas, J.
Thomas, Julian M.
Thomas, Lizzie. *See* Edward, Lizzie Thomas
Thomas, Moroni J.
Thomas, Sarah Ann (Sadie)
Thomas, T.R.
Thomas, T.S.
Thomas, W. Jack
Thompson, Bessie Murk, Mrs.
Thompson, Cordia
Thompson, Dorothy
Thompson, Edgar
Thompson, Edna
Thompson, Hazel
Thompson, Janet
Thompson, John
Thompson, Lillian
Thompson, Orson D.
Thompson, Robert H.
Thomson, Cannon A.
Thomson, Mina
Thomstoft, J., Miss
Thorn, Imogene J., Mrs.
Thorn, Scott Lee
Thorne, Carrie. *See* Patrick, Carrie Thorne
Thorne, Emily
Thornock, LaMont
Thornton, Genevieve
Thornwall, Carl
Thorson, Karl A.
Thorson, Marjorie. *See* Richardson, Marjorie T.
Throckmorton, Gail
Thurman, Claudia Stokes, Mrs.
Thygesen, Henry
Thygesen, Ruth Jensen
Tillbury, Dorothy
Timpson, A.W.
Timpson, G.W.
Timpson, Jean, Mrs.
Timpson, Melba
Timpson, N.S.

Wittwer, Donna
Witzel, E.G.
Witzel, E.J., Miss
Wixey, Annie. *See* Kesler, Annie W.
Wolfgramm, Harold F.
Wolstenholm, Melissa, Mrs.
Wonnacott, Joy, Miss
Wood, Dorothy Marie, Miss
Wood, Elizabeth
Wood, Evelyn
Wood, George C.
Wood, John H.
Wood, Lillian
Wood, Lorena
Wood, Lorreta S., Mrs.
Wood, Mabel. *See* Burton, Mabel Wood
Wood, Marvin F.
Wood, Phyllis
Wood, Rue
Wood, Sarah H., Mrs.
Wood, Sarah L.
Wood, W.
Woodbury, Janice Condie, Mrs.
Woodbury, Joseph Stephen

Woodbury, Melba. *See* Booth, Melba Woodbury
Woodbury, Norma
Woodbury, T.L.
Woodbury, May
Wooley, Ruth
Woolf, Vaneta M., Mrs.
Woolley, A.M.
Woolley, D. Richard
Woolsey, Grace Welch, Mrs.
Worley, Viola (or Veda)
Worley, William R.
Worley, William R., Jr.
Worsley, Ralph
Worthington, Mary
Wraspir, Britt-Marie Bryggman, Mrs.
Wright, Amos
Wright, Clair Ann
Wright, Geneva Ensign
Wright, Genevieve
Wright, Jeralyn Topham, Mrs.
Wright, Lynn Ronald
Wright, M.J.
Wright, Mode

Wunderlich, Esther, Miss
Wynder, Marybeth
Wynder, Max K.

Yank, Susan H., Miss
Yearsley, Karen Adele, Miss
Ylst, Hans
Ylst, Marjo
Yost, Charles
Young, A.P.
Young, B.B.
Young, Barbara Lambert, Mrs.
Young, Betsy Ross
Young, Don C.
Young, E.R., Miss
Young, Emma L.
Young, Eveline
Young, J.H.
Young, James L.
Young, Jeanette, Mrs.
Young, Katheryn, Miss
Young, L.C., Miss
Young, Lillie
Young, Lorenzo S.
Young, Martha Hammond, Mrs.

Young, Marva May Saunders, Mrs.
Young, P.H.
Young, Rettie
Young, Romania. *See* Roby, Romania Young
Young, Ruth O.
Young, S.B.
Young, Sonoma
Young, Wanda S. *See* Olsen, Wanda S.
Youngberg, Florence Cummings
Yuille, Marilyn. *See* Smith, Marilyn Yuille

Zabriskie, Bob Roland
Zabriskie, Grant Rodney
Zackrison, Mary
Zander, Rudy
Zarbock, DeAnne, Mrs.
Zeeman, Kenneth L.
Zeeman, Linda Anderson, Mrs.
Zeender, Margarite
Ziegler, Robert Pingree
Zielke, Lorna. *See* VanKomen, Lorna Z.

Index

Donald A. Rosenfeld
Britt-Marie Wraspir
Helen Weeks
Melvin C. Memmott
John E. Clark
James R. Behling
Stephen A. Bardsley
Marietta Walker
Emma Furness
Beverly O. Pearson
Myra J. Ripplinger
Roland G. Walker
Dorothy M. Ba...
Susan Taggart
James Lawrence Young
Owen D. Pearson
Erik Jensen
Carol Jean Bittner
Wally Wright
Robert Bigler
Robert van Dijk
Don Be...
Jean Ennis
LaVon Rudd
Carol ...
Stella Dowd
Robert Sundquist
Nelson B. Williams
Marion Miller
Patricia Mathis
Julianne Schreiner
Blaine T. Jackman
Hazel S. Perry
Melvin W. Dunn
Oakley S. Evans
Donald H. Ripplinger
Betty J. Hardman
Nancy Lund
Bettie M. Camp
John L. Hommes T-29
Valeen B. Dummer
Alice Swensen
Jon E. Fisher
Virginia B. Sudweeks
Dahlia Moore
Roberta Kelly
Jerold D. ...
Drew Van Wagoner
Blaine Warden
Francis O. Boyer
Gordon ...
Jean Madsen
Marilyn C. Williams
Mary Zackrison
Mary R. Squires
Barbara Byker
Bonnie Robinson
Alice J. Bartholomew
Oralie Waite
William W. Green Jr.
Virginia I. Peterson
Mary Matheson
Lorraine Law
James H. Dawson
Kathy Airmet
Edna ...
Errol ... McCandless
Erlynn B. Leidig
Walter E. McPhie
Eleanor Taylor
Jacquelin Kirkpatrick
Sharon Kimmerat
Brian Whitley
Roberta
Susan Clough
David R. Strang
Dantzel Nelson
Spencer Kinard
The Spoken Word
Vera Espinosa
Stephen Boyd
Jerry Castleton
Donna J. Neal
Dean Vastrup
Kathryn A. Visher
Elfriede Pawker
Robert O. Bennett
Boyd Stuart
Harold L. Gregory
Colleen K. Jones
Richard M. Taylor
Janice Richards
J. Kent Vastrup
Helen Hillier
Carolyn M. Squires
Vern O. Jones
Arnold Pace
Shirley Egan
Cliff Sorensen
Richard N. B...
Amos L. Wright
Gordon Quigley
Darrell J. Brown
Marva Young
Philip J. ...
Darro Hinnemeyer
Richmond M. And...
Gail Meyerhoffer
Robert B. Zigler
Russel Scott
Jean Duncan
Elias Hanno Adams
Kathleen Boyd
Stephen Boyd
Susan Egli
Wendell K. Ward
Donna J. Neal
Clothild Vogenson
Cecelia ...
J. Buchner
Floyd Wm. Neal
Michael L. Pratt
Jessie Tucker
James B. Leonard